T0197240

Autumn

Autumn

THE MANTLE LIFTED

Ronnette Virginia Smith

AUTUMN
THE MANTLE LIFTED

Scripture quotations marked KJV are from the Holy Bible, King James Version (Authorized Version). First published in 1611. Quoted from the KJV Classic Reference Bible, Copyright © 1983 by The Zondervan Corporation

Scripture quotations marked NIV are taken from the Holy Bible, New International Version®. NIV®. Copyright © 1973, 1978, 1984 by International Bible Society. Used by permission of Zondervan. All rights reserved. [Biblica].

iUniverse books may be ordered through booksellers or by contacting:

iUniverse
1663 Liberty Drive
Bloomington, IN 47403
www.iuniverse.com
1-800-Authors (1-800-288-4677)

ISBN: 978-1-5320-5152-4 (sc)
ISBN: 978-1-5320-5153-1 (e)

Print information available on the last page.

iUniverse rev. date: 01/26/2019

AUTUMN

Autumn is ministry through poetry. The book is more prose than poetry. The prose appears after each poem and is accompanied by scriptures. The poems are simple. The prose explains deeper thoughts which evolved by the poetic inspiration.

Autumn is a metaphor following the analogy of seasons. It is to reference fresh breeze blowing in the autumn of life. The season represents experiences that have tested who I am, what I love, and who I believe I was intended to become. As in nature, autumn marks transition from summer to winter, when daylight becomes noticeably shorter and the temperature cools. This a period of maturity. Leaves start to change color from green to yellow, orange to red, and then brown. Finally, the leaves start to fall from trees. They seem to die or dry up like an incipient decline. Quite the opposite—it is actually when trees start to spread their seeds.

These poems don't follow poetic rhythmic qualities of language. The poems are not sonnets. Most of the poems were written early in my life. The poems evolved from a gospel-centered, gospel-minded influence, understanding, and practice.

It is my prayer that seeds planted in these poems will blow in the breeze, fall onto fertile ground, become deeply rooted, and grow up to bear much fruit in the lives of the reader. The goal is to motivate people toward a personal or deeper relationship with Christ—not necessarily to draw to religion (only), but to create a deeper appetite for genuine fellowship rooted and grounded in the Word of God.

In recognition of the fig tree example and expectation of it bearing fruit; everything God made must produce. Let's prepare to produce how God says to produce, when He says to produce, and where He says to produce. We are made for this purpose alone. Mantles, mandates, and callings must be answered, accepted then lifted by faith in God's Word. This will require obedience to, and dependence upon Him. God's favor, restoration, victory and spiritual fruit will be guaranteed (Matthew 25:14-30, Luke 13:6-9, 1 Peter 4:10 - 11).

DEDICATION

Calling

Let everyone with a Calling, be called, and moreover, let's be chosen. If you are gifted, let God package your gift. Let Him brand you. Then, stand in your right positions and callings. The night is far spent, and the day is at hand. Produce Gods fruit (John 15:5-6).

Testimony

Let our Testimony be well done, good and faithful servant (Matthew 25:33). The living God is the giver of life, every gift, and every talent. So, you are gifted. So, what? A gift is just a thing; it can be used, but it should not be worshipped. Gifts used without relationship, fellowship, submission, discipline can be deceptive. It is easy to forget gifts must also operate in God's love. Our goal is to avoid testimony of Luke 13:26-27.

Prayer

Let our Prayer be Lord Jesus Christ get the glory! Mold and bless Your people, God. Establish the work of our hands (Psalm 90:17 KJV).

Charge

Let our Charge be His Charge and purpose regardless of occupation, expertise, field of study, talent, calling, or gift (Hebrews 13:21). Christ came to seek and save everyone lost. Whatever you have, the Lord needs it. Let no rock or mountain cry out in your place (Luke 19:40).

THE MANTLE LIFTED

The subtitle speaks of a mantle. The Holy Bible refers to mantles as forms of clothing or attire. In scripture, mantles usually were lifted up or fell upon people when they were called to duty or ministry.

In 2 Kings 2:9-15, Elisha asked his spiritual father, Elijah, for a double portion of his spirit. Elisha's request would have allowed God's strength demonstrated in Elijah to continue in him. Elijah knew that it would be difficult for this to be accomplished, so he told Elisha only God could perform it. Ultimately, Elisha's request was granted when Elijah was taken up into the heavens. Immediately, Elijah's mantle fell upon Elisha. When it did, Elisha hit the waters at the bank of the Jordon River, the waters split, and he cried out, "Where is the God of Elijah?"

This is certainly my heart's cry. I want more evidence of God to prove Himself as God of the scriptures. Since miracles are performed each moment, it is more accurate to desire people to recognize and identify with the origin. I lift my mantle and ask God for a spirit quickened to action. A double portion. The urgency is now.

> The Lord will perfect that which concerned me: thy mercy, O Lord, endureth forever: forsake not the works of thine own hands (Psalm 138:8–9 King James Version).

> May the favor of the Lord our God rest upon us; establish the work of our hands for us—yes, establish the work our hands (Psalm 90:17 King James Version).

> But we have this treasure in earthen vessels that the excellency of power may be of God and not of us. (2 Corinthians 4:7 King James Version).

For the purpose of this book, my mantle is ministry and proclaiming it through poetry, prose, and scripture.

CONTENTS

BORROWED BREATH

QUICKEN

ANOINTING PLAYS ME

WHAT'S NEXT

PERSONAL NOTES FOR APPLICATION

WHY CHRISTIANITY & SINNER'S PRAYER

LIFT MY MANTLE

As a young girl, I dreamed a dream that shook me. I never forgot it. There was a mantel over a fireplace. It was adorned with a mahogany antique stained mirror. The brick looked established but burnt. Family photos decorated the mantel. Black-and-white photographs of my great-great-grandparents were displayed. The beautiful, talented women posed. Standing at each corner of the mantel were two evangelists. These women were attired like traditionally dressed Pentecostal women. They spoke about the holiness of God. They picked up and examined things off the top of mantel. My immediate family stood innocent as they looked. The scene quickly changed into a blurry, frightful scene. Curses began to be thrown off the mantel, one for each person's weakness. The curses came one after the other with astonishing speed. These curses were arrows and darts thrown with the intention to destroy, or at least it seemed that way. We took off running, and soon we grew tired. *What did we do to deserve this?* I wondered.

All of a sudden, I realized I had power in God's Word to stop the curses. I opened my mouth, and my spirit began to speak. From on high, instruction came like a breeze: "Take the Word of God, strengthen your spirit, and beat each arrow and dart off with the Word of God." My knowledge of the Word of God was minimal, my spirit was slow, and my mouth was muffled. Yet it seemed I was the only one to fight. Floating through the air was a huge mantel that once hung over that fireplace. The mantel was a mantle; it had been hovering, waiting to be taken up and carried. God looks for willing minds and obedient spirits to occupy a place by submission to His will, and to carry any mantle given by Him.

> I am a jealous God punishing the sin of fathers … but showing love to a thousand generations of those who love me and keep my commandments. (Deuteronomy 5:9 New International Version)

After actually experiencing many family disputes and watching the enemy steal things like joy, love, and peace from loving, kind, and gifted people, I knew there was a real problem at the root of our family tree. I have learned that the only help available was through the work of the cross and gained by applying the power and strength of appropriate scriptures.

Christ redeemed us from the curse of the law by becoming a curse for us." (Galatians 3:13 New International Version)

If anyone would come after me, he must deny himself and take up his cross and follow me. For whomsoever wants to save his life, will lose it, but whoever loses his life for me will find it. (Matthew 16:24 New International Version)

Come follow me. Jesus said, "I will make you fishers of men." (Matthew 4:19 New International Version)

I used to be a dreamer. *Autumn* started with my dreams. At first, I wrote all down and sought people to help me interpret. A friend challenged me to start a journal to document prayers, God's Word, and answers received.

God gave grace and added His Word to my dream themes. By doing so privately, I lifted my mantle in Him. This is the public manifestation of it.

FOREWORD

It has been exciting to witness this book come to life. God's breath has been blowing on me for years. Each conviction and poetic expression has come like a fresh breeze.

While writing poems, personal convictions were confirmed. Truth and values in this book are rooted in the Word of God. When thoughts strayed, the Holy Spirit gave correction and focus to properly finish poems.

Jesus said, "God will bring glory to me by taking from what is mine and making it known unto you" (John 16:14 New International Version).

These poems are more than feelings. Mere feelings are not paramount. Man feels many things at various times; any whim can evoke a feeling. The truth about what we feel, think, and act upon is of utmost importance. My references to truth are defined by God's inspired Word, documented in the Holy Bible. God's truth is constant, and His ways are supreme. In my opinion, this truth cannot be better paraphrased than how God breathed it and Jesus became it and lived it out in the flesh as savior of the world (John 1:1–5, 12 New International Version).

The Holy Spirit witnesses, reminds, and guides believers of the truth of God's Word (John 16:7-15). If we were to quantify and analyze the amount of sermons frequent church attendees have heard over a lifetime, it would be difficult to understand why there seems to be minimal application in the life of a believer. The assumptions made here are that God's principles are being taught, received, believed, and obeyed. It is God's intention for His Word to be received, understood, and wholeheartedly relied on.

Believers may not realize how much the Word of God has or has not been deposited within and retained, until situations force them to draw upon it as their only sustenance. Desperate moments reveal it. If there are truths of the Word of God planted in an open heart, it will bring counsel, comfort, guidance, and conviction, yielding many benefits. My prayer for you as a reader is that a reservoir be deposited within you. Draw upon it. I speak this by faith as though it were already completely accomplished within you, the reader, and me in Jesus's name!

"Let this mind be in you which was also in Christ Jesus" (Philippians 2:5 King James Version).

Our thoughts and actions must line up with His Word, not only with the words about spiritual gifts, prosperity, promises of healing, and all of the things that make us look and feel good. Our thoughts must also line up with His character, His ways, His love, His perspective on sin, His desire for His kingdom to come, and His will to be performed, which is not solely or exclusively accomplished in the possession of material things. "God's Kingdom is not a matter of eating and drinking, but of the righteousness, peace, and joy which are gifts and fruits given by the Holy Spirit … for the reign of God is not eating and drinking, but righteousness, and peace, and joy in the Holy Spirit" (Romans 14:17 King James Version).

The kingdom of God is about souls. Jesus suffered so that no person had to die apart from Him. The Bible says the Lord is patient and kind and wants no one to perish, but everyone to repent (2 Peter 3:9). Everything breathing is God's concern. His primarily concern is not ensuring we are happy and carefree. Instead, the kingdom is about bringing all created things unto Himself. God wants every created thing to place its trust and hope in Him and to impart His righteousness. This kingdom coming, and kingdom dwelling lies in Him. He will grant desires of our hearts, which derive from seeking His will. This may include the possession of things, however the center of this joy comes from a union and privilege of being able to call Him Abba Father—that is, our Father. We could acquire no greater riches.

It is a treasured blessing to receive God's Word and to gain the strength to apply it. I pray these poems, thoughts, and grounded scriptures are firmly planted in hearts ready to receive them. My prayer is that you enjoy these poems, but more importantly that you hold firmly to the scriptures. Digest them. Let the scriptures feed and nourish you as

- you admire the Lord, His person, His Word, and His manifold works;
- you see yourself as a fallen being and the Lord as perfection reaching out to a fallen humanity;
- you think on the need to crucify the flesh and realize you cannot do it by yourself;
- you contemplate life's trials, failures, and victories and you ponder meaning in life; and
- you seek purpose in your life.

Among these writings are signature poems. These signatures appear at the beginning of each chapter. Many of my poems were written in the midst of extreme distress and turmoil. In those times, the Holy Spirit completely directed my hand. While writing, I felt like a vessel in which substance was poured. God lifted my spirit. When each poem was finished, I was rejuvenated and assured of His presence regardless of the initial emotion. As I receive these signatures as special gifts, I share them. Other related content is under each signature poem section.

The signature poems are:

- Who Am I? **A Borrowed Breath**
- What Did God Do for Me? **Quicken My Spirit**
- When the Spirit is Quickened, What Does it Do? **The Anointing Plays Me**

TIPS ON READING

Here are some tips on reading the poems:

1. Read introduction & forward

2. Select a title of interest from the Table of Contents

3. Slowly read the poem

4. Determine how/if the poem resonates with you

5. Read the prose (explanation)

6. Use a bible to reference scriptures (any version)

7. Document your thoughts in a journal

ACKNOWLEDGMENTS

To my sister, my original editor. Thanks for listening until I am sure you wanted to burst. May God grant from you evidence of a new heritage He has promised. May we forever bond in God's love and understanding. And may we reach forward for those things which are ahead (Philippians 3:13 -14).

To our parents: Your daughters love you both for respecting one other in ways many divorced parents seem to fall short. You have loved your girls and moved hurts and disappointments in your hearts to ensure we knew it.

Mother: You are a Proverbs 31 woman. You may possibly never know how beautiful you are to me. You showed your daughters an example, great wisdom, tenderness, and forgiveness. We will never let go of your smile lighting up a room. It is my prayer that you experience dancing with songs of deliverance like King David, when the ark of the Lord was returned to the camp (2 Samuel 6:14).

Dad: Thanks for your commitment, your standard of excellence, your love, and your support. During the most difficult times in my adult life, your kindness meant so much. May I never stop reaching for excellence. Always remember when a father or mother forgets or forsakes a child, the Lord Himself promises to take him or her as His own (Psalm 27:10). You are Grace personified. I thank God for His gift of salvation with your name on it.

Evangelist Dillard: Thank you for your example, your teaching, your love, and your prayers. You poured pieces your life in Christ into mine. I appreciate your friendship, and you're always lifting the standard of holiness. You blew into my life such comfort and the winds God already commanded. Forever in my ears will ring "Jesus Christ, whom to know rightly" and "Holiness without, no man will see God." You challenged me to not simply know about God but know Him.

Evangelist Davison: Thank you for your careful submission, example, follow-through, and friendship. You empty yourself out like a vessel to be filled up again for the purpose of giving God's Word to His people. You cry out to God for His people, and it's a beautiful thing! I pray for you as you do for others. "May the Lord bless you and keep you. The Lord make His face shine upon you and be gracious to you; the Lord turn His face toward you and give you peace" (Numbers 6:24–26 New International Version).

To the ministers in my life. Thanks for your examples and obedience to God. I appreciate your outreach, support, and transparency. May manifold blessings fall upon your households. May God plant seeds of everlasting life into your gardens. May God be an everlasting shelter to each of you, as in Psalm 91. May His blood provide an overarching shadow of protection to the generations, churches, and communities you represent.

BORROWED BREATH

BORROWED BREATH

A borrowed breath blowing through this dispensation of time.
A flower bloomed, passing this way once,
Decorated with the colors of springtime.
Sun brightened with the love of summer.
The colors of hazel acorn
Harvested with the pain of autumn.
A fall in full season,
Comprehending all the reasons.
This borrowed breath of mine.
A long life of a day that's beginning is recent as today and whose story has been already told. I dream.
A created vessel whose life has yet to unfold.
As a pupil of the infinite eye in disarray,
A converted lie.
This borrowed breath of mine,
As winter is destined to one day come with its cold, frozen departures of years gone by.
Its purpose revealed is more than to the naked eye.
The journey and all the elements bow with victorious, blood-stained praise.
For simply this borrowed gifted breath of mine.

BORROWED BREATH

This poem represents the essence of life. The inspiration is the brevity of life. Our beginning, of which we know something of the date, time, and who were involved—our parents. Our middle, of which we are living presently. Our end, of which we probably know nothing about except that it will certainly come. "Borrowed Breath" is compared with life's seasons. The underlining theme is the origination of life. The title came directly from Genesis. God blew breath into clay, and that clay man became a living soul. It is prefaced with *borrowed* because our lives are not our own. The clay without the living active, powerful spirit and breath of God would still be clay – useless putty.

God scooped down and blew breath into clay for man to become a living soul. He has not stopped blowing His spirit and provision into, on, and around us to keep us alive. We owe Him because we borrowed.

A stillborn baby is just a body—no life is there. A corpse in a morgue is just a cold lump of flesh—lifeless. Man can build clones and work out every intricate detail like a master architect, but if God does not loan breath, vessels do not breathe. There is no life existence despite any scientific advances. Vessels of clay became living souls due to God's breath blowing. Moment by moment, he blows His spirit of life into us. Indeed, we are living on borrowed breath.

> He is before all things, and in him all things hold together. (Colossians 1:17 New International Version)

> Then the Lord God formed a man from the dust of the ground and breathed into his nostrils the breath of life, and the man became a living being. (Genesis 2:7 New International Version)

> All people are like grass, and all their glory is like flowers of the field; the grass withers and the flowers fades. (1 Peter 1:24 New International Version)

3

BRIDLE ON THE TONGUE

Put a bridle on my tongue.
I sin with it frequently, and it jumps up and out and runs.
It runs circles around those whom I love.
It protects this body I thought was meek and gentle as a dove.
I curse from it and tear people down
Because they hurt me and make my insides frown.
I feel wise when I am doing it and think that I have won.
They pissed me off, I say.
To control this anger is what I desire today.
Turn the enemy's arrows into a joke.
Let me laugh with Your spirit of praise,
Keeping my eyes on You,
Not letting the embers of this anger faze me.
Let Your thinking paraphrase ... would thee?
Lord, please fight my enemies outside and inside—not tomorrow, but today!

Bridle on the Tongue

Did you know that someone who can control the tongue can save his or her soul from danger? Often we respond in error. We tend to go into combat when we do not need to, do not go when we should, or fight in our own strength. Often we try to resolve conflict by attacking or retreating. An uncontrolled tongue starts wars, not just fights. A true test of humility is how one responds when attacked verbally or physically. Sometimes we feel abused, mistreated, or underappreciated. How do you really respond in these instances? Do you really believe God fights your battles? When you decide to fight your own battles, you may discover that you have jumped on someone who is already hurting or is also under an attack. Just because the devil used someone, why let him use you? A man who can control his tongue is victorious.

> No man can tame the tongue; it is an unruly evil, full of deadly poison. With it we bless our God the Father, and with it we curse men, who have been made in the similitude of God. Out of the same mouth proceed blessing and cursing. My brethren these things ought not to be so. (James 3:8–10 King James Version)

> If anyone among you thinks he is religious, and does not bridle his tongue but deceives his own heart, this one's religion is useless. (James 1:26 New King James Version)

PERFORM THY WORD IN ME

In my heart, I feel it.
In my mind, I know it.
From my lungs, I breathe it.
In my belly, I churn with it.
With my feet, I walk it.
From my mouth, I talk it.
My loins are clothed with it.
With eyes, I see it.
Anoint my ears, then I hear it.
With my fingers, I type it.
In my spirit, I yearn it.
From my hands, I lift it.
Placed in my will, I obey it.
With my tongue, I will speak it.
Through my brain, I conceive that He gives, and the Holy Spirit will piece it.
In my tears, I taste it.
With my teeth, I bite it.
From my hurt, He breeds it.
With my soul, I am it.
At night, peaceable I lie because of it—His Word.
In the morning, I wake to sing praises to it—His living Word.
My heart's cry to the Lord.
In Christ, surely He will perform it.

Perform Thy Word in Me

When the Lord said, "I have chosen you," I told Him all about my inabilities as if He did not know it. I told Him I could not do it on my own. He answered me, "I never asked you to." Since that time, my request has been for God to complete the work He started within me.

I ask God: "If I am to do anything, if I have any responsibility, if I am called to any ministry, if I have any gift or talent to use, then, Lord, giver of life, talents, and gifts, please prompt, lead, and guide step by step so my spirit man will be quickened to fully accomplish Your purpose." I believe this to be the only way God's divine will can come forth. He wants us to finish strong (1 Timothy 6:12).

Have you ever stopped to think God knows full well what He is working with when He calls an unequipped man or woman?

I remember representing my corporation as lead sponsor at the Tavis Smiley's America's IAM exhibition in Washington, D.C. Hundreds of African American seniors were coming from all over to see the traveling exhibit featuring the imprint and impact of African Americans on history. When I arrived, I noticed a senior citizen who had arrived at least two hours early for the event. Apparently, she had walked there. Her feet were tired but her spirit was strong. I greeted her, and we talked briefly. I saw her several times before the exhibition opened and the program began. I noticed she watched me. Finally, I went over to talk for a few moments. She told me about herself and asked questions about my life and career. Before I left her presence, she grabbed my hand, looked me straight in the eye, and said, "God prepares those He has already chosen." I looked at her and smiled.

That day, I was asked only to organize and represent professionally on behalf of my employer, but I knew in my spirit that God had much more for me, and He would equip me fully to execute.

Moses gave four excuses and then had the gall to ask God to send someone else before his fifth plea. Read Exodus 4. God answered each excuse with His provision. Even Jeremiah told God he was a child. God told him he must say whatever he was told and go wherever he was sent (Jeremiah 1:5–10). God also instructed Jeremiah as He told Moses, "I have put my words in thy mouth" (Exodus

4:15). God answers every excuse or inability with himself. After a weighty vision, Ezekiel had to receive help from God's spirit to stand, because he had officially been commissioned to preach to the nation of Israel. After showing Ezekiel the depths of rebellion and resistance to be encountered, God continued to pressure Ezekiel. He instructed Ezekiel to open his mouth so He could put His Word in it.

In the book of Ezekiel, God told His servant to hear the word from His mouth and give them a warning. This hesitancy to speak and to obey is common (Ezekiel 2:1–3; Ezekiel 3).

When seeing what it required to redeem humankind, even Jesus Himself, who was fully assured of His perfect union with the Father, had to submit His will (John 10:30; John 14:9). "O my Father, if this cup may not pass away from me, except I drink it, thy will be done" (Matthew 26:42 New International Version).

Scripture tells us their oneness was ordained since the beginning of the world. John 1:1 clearly indicates Jesus and the Father were in complete agreement. Even Jesus Himself found the work He was called to do arduous. He preferred salvation come to man by some other means than by the cross and a breach in their relationship. He did not want to be separated from the Father for even a brief period of time.

Have you been called to do a work? Do you feel less than qualified for it? Has your brand or reputation been tarnished? Have you already embarked upon multiple unfinished works? Have you looked at yourself, your lack of abilities, and your need for discipline or follow-through and said, "there is no way I can do this." Have you surveyed the journey and determined it is too hard to continue? If so, cry out – "Perform Thy Word in Me."

> Being confident of this very thing, that He which hath begun a good work in you will perform it until the day of Jesus Christ. (Philippians 1:6 New International Version)

> And the Lord said unto Moses, Is the Lord's hand waxed short? Thou shalt see now whether my word shall come to pass unto thee or not. (Numbers 11:23 New International Version)

> So shall my word be that goeth forth out of my mouth: it shall not return unto me void, but it shall accomplish that which I please, and it shall prosper in the thing whereto I sent it. (Isaiah 55:11 New International Version)

> And the beauty of the Lord our God be upon us and establish thou the work of our hands upon us, the work of our hands establish thou it. (Psalm 90:17 New International Version)

Make you perfect, stablish, strengthen, and settle you. (1 Peter 5:10 New International Version)

No other foundation can man lay than that is laid, which is in Jesus Christ. (1 Corinthians 3:11 New International Version)

Wherefore gird up the loins of your mind. (1 Peter 1:13 New International Version)

Thy word have I hid in mine heart, that I might not sin against thee. (Psalm 119:11 New International Version)

Then Samuel answered, Speak; for thy servant heareth. (1 Samuel 3:10 New International Version)

GIVE YOU, ME?

Give you, Me? Did I hear you correct?

Are you asking what I suspect?

Give you, Me? How?

Emotionally, mentally, or physically? My spirit doesn't belong to any man, so that's out of the question. I look to the Holy Spirit, and there lies My reflection.

Am I offering precious parts of me without protection? Assurance of longevity?

Or are you even what I want? Is the capture a devastating disappointment from the hunt?

I could say I'm not my own to give, but that would be slightly incorrect, for I've been given stewardship over this camp.

What a responsibility. I sit and think.

Are you, or is anyone else, capable of handling and protecting My fragile emotions? I think not!

Can you conceive My sporadic inventions? Will you support them or perceive them as a threat?-

Do you realize that My body is precious and rare? My satisfaction physically—are you committed to providing with gentleness & care?

Are you aware that two bodies made flesh equal one?

Will you rapture in My love, feel confident with your hold, and then let Me be liberty free? No bondage.

Give you, Me?

Do you know what you're requested? More detailed than suggested—my categories Of interest remain so varied; no burden will be carried.

Give you, Me? Did I hear you correct?

GIVE YOU ME?

This poem is not a bitter reflection. It is an in-depth look at a phrase that a young man spoke without thinking. Then again, he may have given much thought to his proposition but was unable to discern whom he was approaching, or that I would give such a statement substantial deliberation and moral evaluation.

When you grow in Christ, conversations, perceptions, and desires change. Often these changes occur without immediate recognition, yet they come with strong conviction. At times, people take pleasure in seeming profound. In this particular case, a young man offered me a proposition. Someone somewhere may have been flattered. I surmised that he simply did not know what he was asking for, or from whom he posed his request.

Ironically, more than twenty-five years after I wrote this poem, I was awakened and heard the phrase "Give me you." At the time, I had no immediate recall of writing a similarly titled poem. I sat up in my bed and began searching Google with those words. The first thing that popped up was a beautiful gospel song by Shana Wilson entitled "Give Me You." I was anxious to share it. I had been communicating via Facebook with a brother in Christ. I shared it. He told me at that very moment he was listening to the same song.

The lyrics begin, "Give me, you. Everything else can wait. Lord give me, you." The accompanying scripture verses come from 1 John 4:10–20, which finds its root from abiding in God—the fact that He loves us is paramount, not that we proclaim to love Him. It also focuses upon being protected, understanding the difference between the spirit of truth and spirit of error.

The enemy constantly looks for clever ways to trip us up, but God is always there to restore us.

Think about it. God gave us free will to do whatever we want with our lives and bodies. At times, that could be a frightening thought, particularly when you sit and think that our desires are ruled by this flesh. From within our hearts proceed most deceitful intents (Ecclesiastes 8:11; Matthew 15:18–19). We should be asking God to give us Him; everything else and anything else can wait. What God intends is real, best for us, and the truth will be revealed.

When I wrote the poem, if there was any desire or temptation to relish or be amused with his supposition, my spirit enveloped me. I could not even blush for a moment. There was no need to have discussion or look for any deeper thought. Feeling feisty, I wrote a response to his question.

Do you not know that your body is the temple of the Holy Spirit who is in you whom you have from God, and you are not your own? (1 Corinthians 6:19 New International Version)

Can a maid forget her ornaments or a bride her attire? Yet my people have forgotten me days without number. Why trimmest thou thy way to seek love? Therefore hast thou also taught the wicked ones thy ways? (Jeremiah 2:32–33 New International Version)

I have seen all the works that are done under the sun; and, behold, all is vanity and vexation of spirit. (Ecclesiastes 1:14 New International Version)

IF A MAN EXAMINE HIMSELF

The challenge today is:
Will the real Christian stand up?
I submit to you perhaps they wouldn't look like us.
What if their lives are not crowded with conferences or mouths filled with loud spiritual phrases?
They might not carry their Bibles everywhere for others to see.
What if they never protest abortions or speak aloud about rampant, illicit sex and immoral lifestyles?
What if their lives do not look like all the flagrant prosperity that churches teach today?
What if it looks like their children have gone astray?
What if with every pain or hurt, they cannot curse it, and immediately it dies?
What if instead of gleeful giggling daily, often you see tears in their eyes? Who's to
say that those are not tears for you?
Suppose they walk quietly and accumulate many silent victories.
Suppose they stand on a street corner, touching and agreeing in the spirit for every lost soul around
them to be saved, healed, or delivered.
Suppose they hear confusion about how to arise and retreat inwardly to rebuke the devil's lies.
Suppose few people can understand or are even meant to hear their deepest cries,
And they only share cares with the Father beyond the sky.
Suppose when their hearts are broken and everyone knows, quietly people whisper, "Poor soul."
What if they give their cares to God and commit to let the undue burdens and pain go?
Is this person a poor or rich soul?
Suppose the Christian, in God's eyes, doesn't look like you or me. Then with your spiritual
eye, look in the mirror. What is it that you see?

IF A MAN EXAMINE HIMSELF

Use God's Word as an x-ray. Have you ever seen a horror flick where an attractive woman looked in a mirror, only to see a reflection of a frightful distorted monster? I wonder what some of us would see if we looked at a mirror that reflected the intentions and spirits that lived within us?

As an introduction to "If a Man Would Examine Himself," there is a table below with a series of questions. It references self-examination. My father likes to warn that self-examination is dangerous. This is true because the Bible tells us every man is right in his own eyes. In other words, we find ways to justify ourselves. Let's examine ourselves in God's Word; it is the standard. Scripture says judgment will begin at the house of God. It would behoove members of the body of Christ to examine ourselves in the Word. 1Peter 4:17 and 1 Corinthians 1:31 indicate self-examination in the Word of God eliminates the need to be judged by God.

Always think you are right?	All the ways of man are clean in his own eyes. However, the Lord weighs the spirits. (Proverbs 16:2)
Is a heartfelt emotion to be trusted?	The heart is deceitful above all things, and desperately; wicked who can know it? (Jeremiah 17:9) He that trusteth in his own heart is a fool. (Proverbs 28:26)
What is really in the heart of man? Why is it still necessary to ask God for a clean heart once saved?	Out of the heart proceeds evil thoughts, murders, adulteries, fornications, thefts, false witness, blasphemies: these are things that defile man. (Matthew 15:19)
We judge others quickly. Can we also say this about ourselves?	Man looking in a mirror goes away and forgets what manner of man he is. (James 1:24)

Does it feel as if enemies are all around you? If so, you may not be able to change that. Instead, it might be worth examining what is hated or misunderstood?	When a man's way please the Lord he make even His enemies at peace with Him. (Proverbs 16:7) First just before God then just before man. (Proverbs 16:7) Show thyself friendly to obtain friendship. (Proverbs 18:24)
Fearful of man's or God's judgment?	If a man would examine self-he need not be judged. (1 Corinthians 11:31) In God I will praise his word, in God I have put my trust; I will not fear what flesh can do unto me. (Psalm 56:4) The Lord is on my side; I will not fear what man can do. (Psalm 118:6) God is the just judge. (John 5:30)

HE'S NOT MY HUSBAND

As we lay relaxing, I played with your head, counting the number of hairs on your face, examining every pore, every section, every space. Your long fingers slid between mine; we held hands. We didn't kiss much; we pecked once or twice. Lying beside you felt real nice. As I rose up to look you in the face while in a dimly lit room, I noticed you had many moles. I touched each one, awed at the number, and then smiled. He has many beauty moles, I thought. I took time to pick with one or two. You lay there silently; it didn't seem to irritate you. I touched them time and time again as the sun rose; on your moustache my lips fell.

Of your dream, I needed you to open up and tell. I had to hold back, to not crowd you. You blinked, and I saw a tear hidden in your eyelashes. Then I knew why I couldn't sleep. Within my belly, out of it some strength had leaked. We needed so badly to prove that everything was okay and we were still strong. You have nothing to prove to me. Isn't with me where you belong? (What I wanted to say.) As a part of our union, I will accept your strengths, your weaknesses, your joys, and your pains. That's why I can be your helpmate. (The drama of it all.) I'll help refill you, and renewal of purpose you'll gain.

You lay back, quite comfortably in my arms (because I would not let you hold me. I could not keep still), and so I looked at your moles in the light. Suddenly, those beauty moles gave me such a fright. You looked up and saw fear in my eyes. You begged me not to cry. You promised to explain why you let me believe your marks were moles when they were really scars. You're not. We're not. This is just a lie.

HE'S NOT MY HUSBAND

Pretending that something wrong is right is like placing an oxygen mask on the mouth of a cold corpse: it's useless.

Single people are often most unwise, impatient, and disobedient. They seek companionship based upon soulish preferences. This indeed is normal. Many times, momentary comfort is settled for. Single people often work mess into an illusion that perhaps God is pleased with it, will clean up the spills, and will hide secret thrills even from his law or co-sign on enjoying the pleasures of sin for a season. Imagine that!

Inwardly, children of God know God is not pleased, and if hearts are not hardened with disobedience, strength can be recovered. Thank God for continually knocking at our conscience doors to bring remembrance to what is in His will. The pain of it can ache badly, and the weight of it can feel like a ton of bricks. If you have a sense of humor, it is actually comical because often unnecessary anguish is endured. Why not stop straining to blow life into something dead?

This poem is about a relationship. Not for one moment in the quiet of my person did I think, feel, or even want it to be what God intended for my life. Why are we so willing to put up with that which is mediocre at best, planning and strategizing to make it acceptable only to exhaust ourselves?

How long will we dance with the devil and allow that wolf to dress up in sheep's clothing, pamper him, and call a dying, fruitless thing lovely? Why don't we realize that we are prolonging lessons, lying to ourselves, frustrating our purpose, hurting others, and terribly grieving the Holy Spirit.

> Do you not know that he who is joined to a harlot is one body with her? For "the two," He says, shall become one flesh. (1 Corinthians 6:16–17 New International Version)

Flee fornication. Every sin that a man doeth is without the body; but he that committeth fornication sinneth against his own body. (1 Corinthians 6:18 New International Version)

If I make my bed in hell, behold, thou art there. (Psalm 139:8 New International Version)

I HEARD YOU

I know you want a husband. I heard that thought. I swear I did. I feel your weaknesses and have seen what you settle for. You avoid my intimacy and fear My Word. Have you not seen? Or have you not heard? I always hear your deepest thoughts and staggering fears. I see you, and I love you, my dear. I'm so particular about you, you see. I am particular about what you say, what you portray, what you do. Yes, I care about you and what you become a part of, join to, or let join Me and you. I created you with My hand; I am familiar with your frail touch. Yes, I am familiar with your fleshly way, and your most spiritual moments are still next to decay.

I heard you when you asked for a husband. I swear I did. I heard you, and I felt you desire his touch. I love you so much that just anything, just anybody won't do for you. I hear your every thought, your every little whim. I see you when no one is looking and the lights are very dim.

I'll give you what you asked for—I love you just that much. You desire human satisfaction, and that I understand. I created you for My purpose and carved you in My hand. I made your desires and allowed them to be. I want you to reach internally and desire union with Me.

I heard you ask for a husband that piece of clay I made; I brought you out of him. Both of you I love, I made. All I'd really like to know from you two is if you really love Me. When you read My Word, what do you see? Is it just a book of writings, or is it Me poured out on pages and manifested in flesh for all hearts to receive? I hear your every thought, and I can divide the fleshy from the true need. I heard you when you asked for a husband. I said, "I'll give you one, but I have one question I want to know. When you are still thirsty and still feel an inner need when he hurts you deeply, will you forgive him through the power of Me? When you find that no help, no ointment of fleshy man, Christian though he may be, will soothe all that ails you, will you so urgently pray, seek, and long to be touched by Me? I mean, will you then want Me?"

I Heard You

According to scripture, a single Christian woman's desire is to please the Lord, and a married woman desires to please her husband. When I listen to my Christian sisters and women in general, I see a lack of understanding in this paradigm. Many of us want to skip over or simply ignore "desiring to please the Lord" in our singleness. This is unfortunate because there is an enormous amount of peace, comfort, and acceptance in first learning to be submissive to the Lord and giving oneself to Him. Many single women want to rush into finding a man to love and appreciate. We tend to give ourselves fully to things. Then, we expect what we give will be returned. This is understandable because we need and want to be needed. We tend to get it twisted. And, everything seems twisted. We were called to be covered. I have not seen anywhere in scripture women were created to cover. To help, yes but not to cover or lie to ourselves. Increasingly, it seems women are covering to keep appearances. The bible refers to this action as silly minded (Timothy 3:6). Looking at the condition of women all over the world, a woman can become very distraught. Today in many countries, women still do not hold the same rights as men. Often, women are disrespected and even tortured. Be that as it may, in large global numbers women have become very aggressive, successful in business, and hold the same titles as men. Even so, there is still a large gap in how men and women are treated, paid, and valued. The recent #MeToo Movement has brought some of this to light and active discussion.

More and more women have grown to be hyper-independent. Many have elected it by choice, and others have been thrust into roles of serving as mother and father in families, or corporate leaders and owners of businesses. Women are amazing. We are tough, equipped for almost any task, and very efficient.

Regardless of the efficacy of women, we desire companionship. As a matter of fact, men also desire it. Wise advice for the Christian is to embrace who you are in the Lord and seek to become what God desires. One must simply wait for the right person. More important, women and men alike should allow themselves to become the right people. Prior to Eve's creation, God said it was not good for man to be alone, and He decided to make Adam a help to fit him. God took one of Adam's ribs and made woman, and then He brought her to man. Adam named her and proudly announced that they would cleave to one another because they were of the same bone and flesh. After man's fall, God set up a hierarchy that was not in place prior. He let the woman know that her desire would be for her husband, and that the husband would rule over her (Genesis 3:16). This was one of the consequences of Eve's sin. I am not suggesting it is solely a punishment for a woman to desire a man. Rather, it helps to understand why God commanded men to love their wives as their own flesh.

Single women, this poem is for you. Let me make it clear what is meant in its intent. There is nothing unnatural about wanting a husband, nothing unspiritual about wanting to be a wife. The poem intent is to ask, do you fully understand what it is you need and desire? In singleness, have you mastered what God requires? Isn't that preparation for your desire to be a wife? Because the marriage covenant mirrors the relationship between the Lord Jesus Christ and the church, can you adequately submit to a sinful man if you cannot submit fully to a holy God? Do you understand what God requires? I know of many married women who learned only after marriage the blessedness of singleness. I hear God asking if you have first resigned to be his handmaiden?

CONFUSION

A strange state to be.
Things all around, nothing tangible.
Nothing can be found.
A large mess of objects—
No order, just hanging around.
A mind cluttered with thoughts, wishes, doubts, and uncompleted dreams.
Mouth muffled because of many unclean things.
Feet in a swamp, far in desert below.
A maze of mirrors leading no place; where to go?
Arms tied behind your back.
No battle, especially your own, can you fight.
A hunger for foolishness, no end in sight.
Man's unconscious, spiritual plight.
Confusion

CONFUSION

Whether loud or quiet, a man without regeneration is either currently in disarray or in complete bewilderment. Humankind is blessed. Many experts confirm the capacity of our brains and bodies are far underutilized. We are given many talents and abilities. Every baby comes into the world with a blank computer (mind), if you will. From scripture, we know that the carnal nature is already bent from God (Psalm 51:5). Even so, our minds have great capability. A mind can be filled with aspirations, knowledge and solutions. With tenacity and faith, little is impossible.

Many people in overwhelming circumstances have proved it. Yet in the midst of gifts, talents, and making contributions to the world, humans are just dust, mere ashes of confusion, not knowing where we belong and the true significance of our lives. This is the quandary of life from the least to the greatest.

Despite achieving a self or worldly defined summit of success, many accomplished men and women without a relationship with God have shared or something was missing.

The Bible gives a parable of a rich man who accumulated abundance and proceeded to make grand plans to hoard it for himself. God surmised the man was in reality a fool because he was confused about who had actually provided for his life. He obviously was an industrious farmer and had the ability to build, but he lacked one important thing: a most important virtue, an eternal perceptive. He was not in control of his life (Luke 12:16–21). Even Adam and Eve, who lived in a beautifully furnished garden with companionship, friendly animals, and unlimited provision, and who enjoyed dominion over everything, were tricked by Satan, lost perception, and plunged into confusion. They lost a comfortable fellowship with God and with one another. Their fall was accompanied by uncertainty regarding how to view themselves and God (Genesis 3:1–10). Adam blamed Eve, the part taken out of him whom earlier he been delighted with and called her his own body. (Genesis 2:23). Even so, their collective failure changed the course of humanity.

Today, confusion remains the state of humankind without Christ. No fellowship with Him, fear of Him, and insecurity about one's relationship to Him means disharmony with one another and utter confusion, with eternal hell as a destiny.

> There is a way which seemeth right unto a man, but the end thereof are the ways of death. (Proverbs 14:12 New International Version)

> Know ye not, that to whom ye yield yourselves servants to obey, his servants ye are to whom ye obey; whether sin unto death, or of obedience unto righteousness? (Romans 6:16 New International Version)

BACK UP OFF ME—INNER CIRCLE

So you want to heard, seen, and accepted by men? Anyone can be used, so back up off those in the inner circle.

True friends or relatives will never willfully choose to play a part of your demise. But don't be fooled—back up off that inner circle.

You can't tell them everything; they will never understand. Secrets untold, only the Lord Jesus understands.

Those visions that comfort and frighten some, to you He shows; you awaken, and to Him only you should go for the interruption.

You want to lean on a flesh partner to the left or to the right.

No man to lean on, no friend in sight.

"Does he have you hemmed in for his pleasure alone?" you ask.

Only the Father cannot be tempted to trick you, use you, or lead you astray. So why not totally submit to Him today? But even in your submitting, you fall so far short of what He requires for you to be. You cannot do it without Him—can't you see?

You can be influenced by what those whom you trust and love; they say, "You can trust me." Are they committing fully and totally to the Lord in every way, or could the flesh have a hold on their minds, twisting and turning them to cause your or our collective decline?

Even in their most genuine desires to reach into your inner part, beware. Only Jesus should know and bring to light what's in the dark of the inner part of your heart.

BACK UP OFF ME—INNER CIRCLE

In the 1998 motion picture *Hope Floats*, Sandra Bullock, who played Birdie, explained to her daughter, Bernice (played by Mae Whitman) a few things about life. She said, "Beginnings are scary. Endings are usually sad, but it's what's in the middle that counts. So when you find yourself at the beginning, just give hope a chance to float up." Childhood impressed upon me true friendship was hard to acquire and nurture. I changed schools frequently, often in the middle of the school year when friendships had already developed. Over and over as a young girl, I experienced situations like Birdie and the bullies. Thus, I grew not to expect a huge inner circle. I envied girls who seemed to gather lots of girlfriends and sustain close friendships over the years.

Unfortunately, I made what felt like bitter enemies wherever I attended; children who did not care for one another became close allies when they learned they knew me. They may have disliked one another, but they disliked me more. Often rage captured some children so intensely that it frightened adults who observed it. Many underhanded plans were set up for me, so much so that a principal at an elementary school called me into his office to share that the children were against me. Mr. Smith's exact words were, "They are all against you." To add insult to injury, he shared this information with a chuckle and indicated the plot had grown so large that nothing could be done, so whatever unfolded would simply have to happen. His lack of professionalism and empathy led a minister, a family friend, to call the police, and a civil rights group intervened. I lived much of my childhood in fear of confrontation. My stomach was always nauseous around mischievous children. I was not afraid to fight, but I did not prefer it.

This trend followed me to college. My freshmen year was very difficult. I envied girls who could make and retain friendships, although I had been accustomed to not doing so myself. I would be nice to people, but there was only so far that I would go with them and let them go with me. I didn't trust them, and obviously they didn't trust me.

Those experiences, though very painful and unfortunate, allowed my trust and relationship with the Lord to grow deeper and richer. I found in Him a true and consistent friend, and God fought all the battles I did not instigate.

Once during a church choir rehearsal, a group of girls sat in the back of church. They whispered and discussed a plot, but I overheard the plan. One of them was to lure me into the bathroom for a fight. The intro to the conflict was to go something like, "I heard you said …" The girls involved one by one walked out of the back of the sanctuary. My supposed friend was the one assigned to lure me to come to the restroom for something. She did. I sat completely still, looking forward. I talked to God in my own way and shared with Him how tired I was of fighting. My stomach churned. I was not necessarily scared, but I was tired of fighting.

I felt I heard a voice clearly instruct me, "Do not move." My little friend continued to press, coming up with all types of ideas to lure me that direction. I didn't even look her way. She must have thought I was mute or crazy. Within minutes, just like a Jehoshaphat experience, there were screams and much ruckus coming from the restroom. The plotters had turned on each other (2 Chronicles 20:11-12, 23-24). Oddly enough, some of them were even related. The adults were baffled. Choir rehearsal ceased, and the spankings began. As for me, I got up and walked past them to the phone hanging on the wall to call my mom and tell her choir rehearsal was over. She was working in my grandmother's beauty salon. Upon arrival at the salon, I shared with them and their patrons how God had fought my battle. I could see they were greatly encouraged to see God show up like that. From time to time, my mother and sister still mention how God moved on my behalf that day.

My desire for a large inner circle has decreased significantly. After experiencing life and looking at the Word of God, I found that often those very close to you are able to deeply hurt you. At first it was comforting to see that it appeared Jesus Christ had only an inner circle for the purpose of training for the Gospel. His life showed complete fellowship, and trust with God the Father was paramount.

If you have had or are having similar experiences as my childhood, let me urge you to examine yourself (Proverbs 16:7). When I examine the Lord's personality, I realize that He was completely open and vulnerable to mankind, not to satisfy them or gain popularity or their favor. After all, Jesus knew their hearts, and still He was committed and confident in His mission. Jesus knew His identity. His vulnerability and openness was completely wrapped in His relationship to the Father. This was the character God formed in Him, in line with His purpose for mankind.

When disappointed by people, I learned to turn to God and tell Him. This habit became my refuge and comfort. What I did not recognize was that my thoughts were, I love only You, Lord! Not them! God allowed me to continue this for quite some time. Finally, He impressed upon me it was time to grow up—and grow up not only naturally but also spiritually. The isolated, self-absorbed refuge was no longer acceptable. It was then that God began to teach me to pray for those who misused me, rather than ignore their existence. In this process, God helped me to see more clearly those whom I did not treat fairly in their attempt to befriend and love me.

Years ago, I used to hear stories or testimonies of homosexuals hiding in the church so as to not be found out, as if it was not visible or apparent to a discerning eye. The fact is many people are hiding different things, or so they think. I think one wise thing to do, as I did, was hide my relationship hurts in Christ. The scripture does say, "Cast thy care upon the Lord for he cares for you" (1 Peter 5:7). It is important to know that Christ is not just a burden bearer but a healer and a deliverer. He does not simply cover us. He reveals us and makes us see ourselves. He also cleanses and heals us. You can hide in Him, but you cannot hide from Him. Jesus is not in the business of covering your sins or hurts for camouflage's sake. He is not in the business of protecting our image. He uncovers, addresses, covers, cleanses, and continues to develop. He completely heals.

Now, whenever I whisper, "I love you," to the Lord, He answers me as he did Peter: "If you love me, feed my sheep" (John 21:15). He used to simply comfort and assure me. Now, it seems He points me to others He loves. The Holy Spirit also brings back to remembrance that His Word tells us we cannot say we love God, whom we have not seen, and not love our brothers and sisters, whom we see every day. Let me pause and self-disclose. I have never hated an enemy so badly as to want to harm the person, but not loving without all inhibition is not love.

I still struggle with inner circles. I have found good friendships build strength and character and add perspective. "As iron sharpens iron so one man another" (Proverbs 27:17). Even so, if not checked my natural response is usually, "Back up off me!"

This poem comes from lack of trust, which is not a good place to reside. It is important to note that one can only truly lean, depend on, and trust the Lord. The devil knows how to cleverly twist things. Keeping people at bay to a certain extent can be a comfort. Even so, it can be an unhealthy behavior if not done with temperance and balance. It has been a great comfort to know even Jesus had few intimates. Even so, this truth should not be used as a crutch. Even as Jesus was perfectly attentive to his heavenly Father's will, He saw mankind completely in our corruptible state and filthy intentions. His focus remained on the work He was sent to perform. This work was obedience to the Father, redemption of mankind by forgiveness through His sacrificial death on the cross – this took agape love, vulnerability, and giving all of Himself. God was simply hell bent on pursuing peace with mankind.

Lord take us to a place where we have no dependence on man but place our trust completely in You to be a light and exude Your love so that we can walk among enemies, be open to whatever they deliver, love them despite it. In the process, teach us to become friends and gain some committed to sharpening lives, mirroring Your fulness, love and forgiveness.

As a Man Thinketh, so Is He!

Just because I didn't say it, I thought it in my mind.
I told them off—oh, yes, hundreds of times.
I sized him up and ranked him low.
I boxed him and hit with many blows.
Yet I thought I was justified and doing okay,
'Cause I refrained the evil word to say.
Yet I thought it in my mind.
I ranked her very low.
I hit her in the face.
Blow by blow, I brought her low.
I thought she was stupid and very unwise.
I took her down, brought her down to size.
No one heard it. I thought I won. I get tired of being the beat-up one.
So I didn't say a word, just kicked real low and
shrunk myself, blow by blow.

As a Man Thinketh

I think; therefore I am.
—Rene Descartes

Often we fight and wrestle with the anticipation of victory. For the direct, they fight upfront, loud, and personal—very combative. For the passive-aggressive, sometimes they fight with games, tricks, and schemes. These methods are useless to a committed Christian. Ephesians 6:12 tells us that the warfare is not against flesh and blood, but against principalities, powers, rulers of darkness of this world, and spiritual wickedness in high places. It further explains to the believer that the appropriate equipment to put on is the "whole armor of God." This is learning the truth of the Word of God, standing on that truth, speaking that truth, praying and demonstrating faith in the truth, and accepting the work of cross on our behalf (Ephesians 6:13–18).

It is easy to focus on what others do to offend us. Dealing with ourselves and our thoughts is frequently overlooked. The battlefield is in the mind with imaginations and thoughts. What are you meditating upon? Just as the word of God is planted like a seed, sinful thoughts are also planted first in the mind. After being cultivated, either they manifest physically through an outward act, or they simmer, eventually contaminating the spirit.

When the Word of God is read, received in faith, and meditated upon, it will renew the mind and transform to the likeness of Christ (Ephesians 4:23–24). It is important to watch your thoughts. Simply because you lean to silence in a situation doesn't mean there is not war raging within you. What we entertain is what we become—as a man thinketh.

MY INNER CIRCLE

Jesus is a melodious tone. In the wee hours of the morning, I feel the oil of joy drip in my heart,
seeking to massage it from its bitter parts.
You are the inspiration that gives me hope.
If I meditate on You, my sadness and distressful moments don't need fake highs or dope.
Cool folks can think I sound corny or like a nerd,
But alone in Your presence, I feel free as a bird,
And I feel in love.
The warmth all in my heart soothes and claims all that hurts in the inside parts.
These moments, I wish could be forever,
And that I never remember any thrill that the world
deceitfully drills as being coveted.
Never let me forget this moment,
How sweet.
Move all around me world.
You are forever outer.
This is my inner,
Which I come home to;
In it must I dwell.

My Inner Circle

In His presence is fullness of joy.

A beautiful love scene inspired this poem. Not the type of scene we identify with on film or in our natural lives—one even more beautiful and meaningful. We long for affirmation: to be loved, to be treasured, to be touched, to be known, and to be unconditionally accepted. Well, the Lord does just that, and so much better than man or woman. We should desire and embrace more fellowship with the Lord with an expectancy of true fulfillment. Truly He can visit us. He visits and touches, satisfies completely, and feels better than any human touch.

Let me clarify: I am not speaking of some romantic experience with spirits, or some love affair with God on our terms or in a fleshly or spiritually twisted imagination. I am speaking of an experience devoid of fleshly outreach or spiritual uncleanness. What is referenced here is agape love for corruptible humankind, where you realize who you are and who He is.

> For I am persuaded that neither death nor life, nor angels nor principalities nor powers, nor things present nor things to come, nor height nor depth, nor any other created thing, shall be able to separate us from the love of God which is in Christ Jesus our Lord. (Romans 8:39 King James Version)

> He brought me to the banqueting house, and his banner over me was Love … His left hand is under my head and his right hand doth embrace me. (Song of Solomon 2:4 King James Version)

INSPIRATION FLOWS

Man schemes his way, but the Lord directs his path.

If the world is a mountain of problems, then ask the one who framed it.

Ask the one who set boundaries for the seas and borders to enlarge them for their necessary capacity.

Ask the one who spoke light into existence and set the night for the resting of all.

Ask the one who flung the stars into the skies and does not allow the sun or moon to fall out of its space, but establishes its boundaries through holy rules and the law of gravity, light and darkness accompanying their rightful time and place.

Ask the one who molded man's mental capacity.

The one who scooped down into clay and blew the breath of life into clay.

The one who even Satan and evil forces must answer and give an account to.

The one who makes them very keenly aware of their scope of influence and final destiny.

Woman can be help.

She was made to, taken out of man to assist in ruling; this is true.

But watch from whence her wisdom originates, for she initiated the Fall.

She can be the stronghold that propels you to a more righteous destiny, or she could be one used to craftily weave a web of deceit.

And depending upon her strength and what her eyes desire and ears perceive, her best intentions can sweetly caress you both to sleep.

So when seeking her and recognizing her dubious role, make sure your final answer and decision does not deviate from what you have been told.

Because the Lord made you the stronger vessel, and because you were lonely, she came along.

She was made to fit you, but don't allow her to make you sin.

Together, you were meant to take back what the enemy stole; the two of you were meant to walk in the breeze of day with unhindered fellowship, with the Father enjoying the day.

INSPIRATION FLOWS

While on a business trip, a young man caught my attention, shared his dreams, and talked about some of his inventions. He was very intelligent and talented. I was impressed and agreed in my spirit that all he desired and what he laid his hands to would be successful. Even so, I knew despite gifts and talents, he needed the Lord to move on his behalf. I listened intently to him. I shared little except that I wrote poetry. He asked for poem. I told him I must be inspired to write, though immediately I was ignited. Within hours, many things came to mind. I penned a few thoughts, and some were enticing. Quickly reprimanding myself, I thought about how women can be used. My flirty thoughts were not important to share. What I wanted to give had to be something that would last, something special.

Suddenly, I remembered my mother challenging me as a young, hormonal girl to write things special and not just ordinary things every teenager could feel, experience, and write. This man's mind drew me. With great effort, I strained not to fall in love and set up my own fantasy. It was then, as if by a heavenly wind, God handed me a platter with the following women's names on it.

Eve—Adam's wife, lusting after what looked good to the eye

Potiphar's wife—used as an enticer

Delilah—deceitfully tempting, relentless, looking for weakness in the strong man Solomon

Vashti—in book of Esther; decided she was going to disobey her king and do her own thing

I whispered to myself, "Give him something to make him strong." Then I penned this poem. Before I wrote it, the Lord let me know it would be beautiful. As confirmation, upon hearing it, he stated it was the most beautiful poem he'd ever heard. I assumed he had probably never read or heard any poetry before. I agreed and smiled because it was a confirmation that the Lord had bestowed His grace upon my writing. I was grateful to be able to give him something that would encourage and strengthen him. And in the years to come, it would reflect the integrity of the writer.

QUICKEN

QUICKEN MY SPIRIT

Quicken my spirit, so I can hear You and obey at the moment of truth.

Don't let me get use to Your love and respond aloof.

Don't let me get use to Your tug on my heart.

Please don't use me to help deliver others

And let the enemy tear me and mine apart.

Don't let me be a voice that cries and screams out Your name, and not be able to practice or to live out Your life, professing You in vain.

Don't let the house You have picked and built for me be positioned on a hill in vain.

Don't let me stand before You in shame.

Only You have the power to present me faultless,

And only You enable me to type this melody of words I write for You.

I love You, Jesus. Don't let me be a hypocrite.

QUICKEN

Dr. Abraham Maslow, a renowned psychologist famous for developing the hierarchy of needs, coined the term *self-actualization* as the pinnacle that human beings strive toward in life. Beyond particulars of air, water, food, and sex, he laid out five broader layers: physiological need, need for safety and security, need for love and belonging, need for esteem, and need to actualize self, in that order. In other words, to know you exist and be given the instinct to survive, as well as to give and receive love, are primary, but realizing yourself and becoming acquainted with yourself and your maximum potential is what completes the sum of humankind's needs.

Although Dr. Maslow was brilliant with worldly wisdom, there is still a greater actualization. Man needs a savior regardless of the level of education. Education is important to maneuver and operate naturally, but only God can truly satisfy a man's thirst for purpose and fulfillment. Because Maslow cannot speak for himself any longer, we are not sure whether the third need he listed—the need for love and belonging—was an acknowledgment of needing God's love and a relationship with Him. What we do know according to scripture is when God created man, He said it was not good for man to be alone, and He made him a helpmate (Genesis 2:18). We also know that even with companionship and all provision for life cared for, both Adam and Eve sinned. God Himself demonstrated more than anything that they needed help to atone for their sins, and so He made provision for cleansing (Genesis 3:22; Hebrews 10:5). Just as man and woman were left to themselves to discover what might satisfy, they messed up, and all else had to be adjusted.

All men are born in iniquity and shaped in sin; therefore our awareness is selfish and self-centered from the beginning. To identify the self is not hard; simply observe fleshly men as Maslow did. The world's ideality and treasure is full of self! The irony involved is deeply rooted in self and selfishness.

In our naturalness, we perceive that taking care of self is all we need. In other words, if we are existing well, feel comfortable and secure, have satisfying relationships, feel good about our image, and are successful in our fields of interest, then we have it made. These things mentioned are nice to possess, and we need many of them for healthy esteem. Yet these things are temporal and highly dependent upon unpredictable circumstances. For the believer (a Christian) to self-actualize is to recognize that what the Word of God says is true about all men. That is, self-reality is carnal, fleshly, and corruptible in nature. Self-nature is bent away from God. This knowledge affirms that in the flesh, regardless of abilities, position, or knowledge, we cannot please God (Romans 8:8). Also, pleasing man or pleasing ourselves will ultimately prove futile (Matthew 16:25–26).

Every need man had been given by God was meant to be supplied by Him. Our potential is wrapped up in seeking His will. Focusing upon self has everything to do with the person seen outwardly and accomplishments of the person alone. The body is simply a representative here on earth. The shell in reality is like grass and a fading flower (Psalm 103:14–15). Knowing this is true self-consciousness.

Our whole identity lies in the Lord. Who did he intend us to be become? What potential did he place within? Are we tapping into that potential? To what degree have we submitted our will to His to accomplish it?

Let me ask you to participate in two activities. One requires a mirror. The other requires a resume or a biography. If you have neither, jot down a list of your life accomplishments—things that make you proud.

Activity 1. Get a mirror. Take a few moments to admire yourself. If you don't admire anything, look intently anyway. Now, regardless of your outward appearance, ask yourself if there was nothing but a vapor of dusty air in front of you, what portion of that vapor could be grasped or retained?

Activity 2. Write a list of your accomplishments. Review them quickly. Take a moment to gloat and think upon how wondrous you are. Regardless of the productivity of your natural life ask yourself if you are stripped without utensil to write. What would be the value of that paper?

You cannot grasp a vapor. There is no value in presenting a blank sheet of paper. Let me ask several other questions before moving ahead.

Do you feel your spirit man is alive in Christ? Are you alive or dead to spiritual things? Are you walking in light or darkness? In your day-to-day activities, do you walk in darkness or light? What types of things do you meditate upon? What takes up most of your time? Because your body will certainly decay, become dust, and completely vanish. Where will your spirit live for eternity (Hebrews 9:27)? And because heaven and earth will pass away according to scripture, what is the meaning of your accomplishments? What, then, is the self, actually?

I ask God to quicken the spirit, make it alive in Him, strengthen it, and make us real. Truly, the spirit is willing but the flesh (this self) is weak (Matthew 26:41).

> Behold, I have longed after thy precepts: quicken me in thy righteousness. (Psalm 119:40 Kings James Version)

> Consider how I love thy precepts: quicken me, O Lord, according to thy lovingkindness. (Psalm 119:159 Kings James Version)

In the Blood

It's your type,
Gives DNA further insight.
Red cells,
White cells
Appears blue in veins,
Flowing through my brain.
Its oxygen
Lining my womb, preparing for life,
Shed in strife.
Even disease feeds upon it to breathe and live.
To kill disease and cut off the blood supply.
To share organs blood types must match, or the body will reject, simply detach.
There must be a oneness in fellowship.
Though the blood must breathe, it must inspect.
If it drains, the vessel is left dead and cold.
For true life-giving blood I am sold.
Blood rushes to a wound to begin healing the damage and hurt.
Fed intravenously to prevent life-giving power from deserting the heart.
In the blood is where life begins. Where sin is cleansed—where redemption is purchased—where heritage is established
This is where a spirit man without truth can remain apart.
Without Jesus's blood, Israel's door was left uncovered.
Their example, and opening if we take no advance, will leave us perverted.
For the blood can graft us all in, and still procure this restoration.

IN THE BLOOD

Mysteries remain about the blood that flows through our veins, yet we know its many functions. Scientists have uncovered what the Lord demonstrated and told us millennia ago: that all provisions for life are in the blood. Blood has been significant throughout the ages. For example, the Old Testament tabernacle set an example of things to come. It mirrored heavenly things and criteria for earthly worship.

Under the old covenant, the high priest entered the tabernacle and went into the Holy of Holies once a year to make sacrifice for people's sins only after he had made atonement from his own sin. This was done through sacrifice and shedding of blood. Hebrews 9:22 confirms that "without the shedding of blood there is no remission of sin." The high priest's work included shedding the blood of bulls, goats, or sheep. The animals had to be in their purest form with no noticeable blemishes. The observance was a foreshadowing of the redemptive work of the cross, which represented Jesus Christ, the Lamb and fulfillment of Old Testament types. This type of lamb, Jesus Christ, was without blemish, shedding His blood for all humankind once and for all. His sacrifice of life was the only effectual and permanently acceptable blood. No animals or other human beings could do it. He was perfect, knew no sin, and was without any blemish on the inside or outside. Because He knew no sin, He became sin for us. He carried man's sin and paid the debt man owed to God the Father. Therefore, our victory is always found in the blood of Christ Jesus (Hebrew 9:7-28; Hebrews 10:1-20). Our spiritual lives are procured by the blood.

Without blood that flows through the veins, the body would not have life. Thinking about the natural function of a menstruation cycle, when a woman's body functions properly, every month the lining of the uterus fills and thickens, preparing to develop, nurture, and protect life. If there is no sperm, penetrating of egg, blood stored will release because there is no life there to sustain. Thus, the woman's body simply purges itself.

During menopause, a woman's cycle ceases, and there is no blood because the time of child bearing is past; life can no longer be nurtured.

Take any sample of blood for any purpose, and if contaminated in anyway, natural life is in danger. Life is in the blood, and the purity of that blood determines the longevity and the health of that life. Through Jesus Christ's unblemished blood. We have abundant life. God gives us some great parallels in life for learning and understanding. Spiritually and naturally, life is in the blood.

> For the life of the creature is in the blood. (Leviticus 17:11 New International Version)

> Without shedding of blood is no remission. (Hebrews 9:22 New International Version)

> But when Christ came as high priest of good things that are now already here, he went through the greater and more perfect tabernacle that is not made with human hands, that is to say, not a part of this creation. He did not enter by means of blood of goats and calves; but he entered the Most Holy Place once by his own blood, thus obtaining eternal redemption. (Hebrews 9:11–12 New International Version)

MATTHEW 15:8

I examine myself in an age when I have to ask, "Will the real Christian stand up?"
Everyone wants to show you how to get something from God or how to claim promises and gifts;
you're entitled to them because you claim to be a Christian.

This focus somehow seems to be still on me, on you, and how we can get or achieve.
Now, tell me how is this different from worldliness, from astrology or even witchcraft?
My focus is on my flesh and how the desires of my three best friends Me, Myself, and I can be met.

How different is this Christianity the whole world seems to profess?
When I fast, it is because I want His attention? Am I not His invention?
Does He not know my intention?
When I seek to deny this flesh, is it not to put Him to the test
To see if He gives something better based upon my appetite?
Because God's stamp of approval is on me (because of Jesus's shed blood), does He cater to my
whims, make me rich, prosper my hand, and snap His finger at all I profess?
As I examine myself, what a scary state we seem to be in,
Professing much and knowing better how to sin with great sophistication,
Vainly babbling through much biblical talk.
#Hashtags and tweets—wiser but weaker, and relationship deletes.
What about this Christianity today?
Talk about much of nothing!

MATTHEW 15:8

We praise God with our lips, but are our hearts far from Him? In an age when it seems everyone professes Christianity, there seems to be such contradictions in character and behavior. There are favorite messages: "Name it, claim it." "Speak the Word, and it shall be so." Faith messages of prosperity and more herald from many a stained-glass window and church corridor.

An evangelist once explained to me God's people are being taught to defraud Him. Often they are claiming promises to which they have not met the requirement. The requirement is faith. For an onlooker who is really trying to see Jesus, looking at modern Christianity could be a huge stumbling block. We often say all the appropriate things, quote the right scriptures, research and cross reference biblical history to exercise gifts, and claim prophetic anointing. But will we be found as nothing more than sounding brass? Will we be found an enemy of the cross? (See Philippians 3:17–19.) Are we following God for the fishes and loaves? "Help Lord, the godly man ceaseth" (Psalm 12:1 King James Version).

> For everyone looks out for his own interests, not those of Jesus Christ. (Philippians 2:21 New International Version)

> But seek first the kingdom of God and His righteousness, and all things shall be added unto you. (Matthew 6:33; Philippians 2:21 New International Version)

> From the least to the greatest of them, all are greedy for gain; prophet and priests alike, all practice deceit. Peace, peace, they say, when there is no peace. (Jeremiah 6:13–14; Philippians 2:21 New International Version)

> These people honor me with their lips, but their heart is far from me and in vain they worship me. (Matthew 15:8–9a New International Version)

WORKS OF THE FLESH—MY ENEMY!

Deliverance, I need you. Help me to seek you in spirit and in truth.

Take the lying spirit away. Create in me a clean heart today.

Inspire me to think and put thoughts together,

For I cannot dare think on a good thought without you.

You are all over me.

In my weakness, please, Lord, hold me.

In my evaluation, when I am close to You, I am still far away.

You said that there is none that seek You. I need Your deliverance. How can I help and do the things You have called me to do when me, myself, my ways are so far from You?

I am grateful You came, causing the wedge Satan made so far—bridged.

I thank You, Jesus, for being the bridge created in God's heart.

Here on earth, I desire the treasures and peace therein.

Search far and wide and have found no friend, reaching deep inside trying to be one myself, wretched ball of clay.

To be a friend one needs, I need Your help. I seek my desires and to satisfy this flesh of mine.

To think of others, my whole self declines.

Drink a glass of water to quench my weary soul—how can I be so young yet feel so very old?

I say this state I don't deserve, but my plight You have on reserve.

When a loving mother who normally had all the answers, eyes and smiles seem to fade – far away, oppressed and disturbed by random voices, exclaiming, "they say". This place is full of troubles, yet many want to stay harassed by the enemy and play in flesh works.

Glimpsing at the sun makes me know I am not alone—inside with You is my eternal home.

I need—we need—Your deliverance.

WORKS OF THE FLESH—MY ENEMY!

It's hard to believe that you are sleeping and living with an enemy, right? Believe it. Are you a believer? Have you been redeemed by the blood of the Lamb? Have you been sanctified (set apart for God's purpose)? Have you been filled with the Holy Spirit as identified by the Pentecost experience in Acts? Do you believe that holiness is still right? Are you sure of your salvation based upon the Word of God? Are you convinced of Calvary's efficacy? If all your answers are yes, then praise the Lord for His glorious works.

In spite of your stabilizing belief in the efficacy of Christ, this message is to remind you there may still be issues and areas that our heavenly Father may be pointing to, even as I write and you read. Some issues may be known, and others may be unseen for now. One thing is for sure: we need His continual deliverance from the works of the flesh.

> Surely, I was sinful at birth, sinful from the time my mother conceived me. Surely you desire truth in the inner parts, you teach me wisdom and in the inmost place. (Psalm 51:5–6 New International Version)

> I do not understand what I do. For what I want to do I do not do, but what I hate, I do I. And, if I do what I do not want to do, I agree unto that the law that it is good. As it is, it is no longer I myself who do it, but it is sin living in me. I know that nothing good lives in me, that is, in my sinful nature. For I have the desire to do what is good, but I cannot carry it out. For what I do is not the good I want to do; no, the evil I do not want to do—this I keep doing. What a wretched man that I am! Who will rescue me from this body of death? Thanks be to God—through Christ Jesus our Lord. (Romans 7:15–20, 24–25 New International Version)

SEEKING WHOM HE CAN DEVOUR

The serpent's eye.
I had a dream a snake was wrapped around the bottom of my legs.
Quickly I shook him off and kicked his head.
Soon I felt it nestling against me again. I moved;
It jumped and hissed.
It was ugly, then it began to pop, and wherever I went, it followed.
It disguised itself as a pretty poodle, and when I looked close, it appeared so unclean.
It was a weak, dying, pitiful thing.
I tried to save it and then later ignored its pestilence presence.
I turned my back, and it became an alligator, quickly twisting and turning.
I looked back twice, and there were more swimming around in a swamp.
I thought that if I fell in, they would quickly devour me up.
They came from everywhere, and how terrible—uck!
I kept escaping their presence, but always, always they were on my track,
Trying to get me when I turned my back … but I didn't feel like fighting.
Now, I am getting tired of that serpent's eye—his defeat is foretold, and that's no lie.
So he'll try and try to tear me down; he wants to kill and beat me down.
Why? 'Cause I've got a press for righteousness, mine eye on the prize.
He wants destruction bad, but the fact is, Satan, the Lord Jesus Christ rebukes you!
I love Jesus, and He has not rejected, refused, denied, or cursed me; my future is
guided by my Lord's guiding eye.

SEEKING WHOM HE MAY DEVOUR

We have to keep our eyes open, both our natural and spiritual eyes. This is to suggest coherence, not paranoia. Remain awake and alert! God allows nothing to come upon a listening, watching, and obedient servant unaware. The Word of God says that our adversary roams around, seeking whom he may devour (1 Peter 5:8). This indicates our enemy's mission but also his limitations. The enemy is agile chaos on the run. He seeks whom he may devour, yet his destination remains; defeated foe.

Peter's exhortation reminds us Satan may not cause destruction anywhere he desires. When God asked Satan in Job 1:7 what he was doing, our adversary responded, going to and fro walking in the earth. Satan was anxious, mischievous and seeking who and where he might steal from or devour. God recommended His servant Job because He knew Job respected Him, hated evil, and would remain faithful. Before pouncing on Job, Satan complained and protested to God that He had a hedge of protection around Job so that nothing could be done to him. God had to lift that hedge before Job's adversary could attack him.

We feel everything is fine as long as our bills are paid, our families are healthy, and we know no serious tragedies. If everything seems to be moving smoothly, all is well. Lack of knowledge in God's Word lulls us into spiritual complacency. My people suffer because of lack of knowledge (Hosea 4:6). If you know and serve the Lord, you are one of Satan's targets. He hates God the Father, Jesus the Son, and you—a joint heir (John 15:8). By the way, if you have no desire to know God, Satan still hates you. And, you are right where he wants you—lost, deceived, and lost without God's promise of protection (2 Corinthians 4:4). In the book of Revelation, John wrote about Satan's fall from heaven and his work on earth: "That old serpent, called the Devil, and Satan, which deceived the whole world...woe to the inhibitors of the earth and the sea...? (Revelation 12:12 KJV)

FALLING AWAY

Love covers multitude of sins.
Iniquity shall abound.
The love of many shall wax cold.
Many shall be offended,
Passive aggressive.
Sensitivity,
Flesh an enemy.
Church has joined the world.
Many shall be offended.
How can preachers who say they love you turn away and let you go?
Pray for the ministries who need strong Christians to lift up their hands.
What movement is popular today?
Follow man, apostle, or your way.
Many shall be offended,
Passive aggressive.
Sensitivity.
Strengthen up inner man, say, "I am offended."
Get it right.
Get it straight.
Short is the day. Show us the right way.
Reduce by significant kingdom numbers those who fall away.

FALLING AWAY

Woe to the shepherds that feed themselves but do not feed the flock. The diseased have not been strengthened, the sick have not been healed, that which is broken has not been mended neither have they looked for those that strayed away and are lost.

—Ezekiel 34:2–4 New International Version

Ever heard the prophecy that there would come a time when people would fall away from the faith? I must confess I have wondered how this could be possible if people really once believed. Read 2 Thessalonians 2:3–6, 1 Timothy 4:1, 2 Timothy 4:3–4, and 2 Peter 3:17.

The Bible clearly warns about keeping spiritual composure in the wake of the second coming of Christ. The apostle Paul wanted to ensure believers would not be deceived. He desired them to recognize the spirit of the anti-Christ and to be assured this spirit would be revealed before the coming of the Lord. He pleaded for believers to be spiritually awake to perceive and understand the condition of the body of Christ prior to the Lord's actual return.

The question remains: How could one believe, have faith, be committed to fellowship with the Lord, and all of a sudden fall away from that commitment? Hebrews 11:6 comes to mind: "for he that cometh to God must first believe that he is." Then there is a big indicating imperative to also believe God is a rewarder of they who diligently seek him (Hebrews 11:6). This denotes continued faith. This walk of faith means following Christ and His earthly life of obedience and perseverance. Jesus taught converted Jews in this way: "if ye continue in my Word you will be my disciples indeed" (John 8:31). Knowing the truth and accepting it is a first step, but following in that truth is what leads to a sustained fellowship.

After initial saving faith in Christ Jesus, there must be diligence and perseverance to hold on to faith. "Faith comes by hearing and hearing the word of God" (Romans 10:17). The word of God must be planted in the heart, affirming an eternal reward and the belief of benefit. This motivates a wholehearted following of the ways of Christ Jesus. It's not the mere following of faith, promises, miracles, revelations, or demonstrations.

Remember that the devil is a deceiver and master of delusion. Spiritual activity, involvement, or confession alone is not faith; neither are those activities alone works of which God has approved. If it were so, why would Jesus indicate that in the end-time, many would say to Him they prophesied, cast out devils, and did wondrous works in His name, and He would in turn reply, I never knew you; depart from me, ye that work iniquity" (Matthew 7:22-23).

"I never knew you: depart from me, ye that work iniquity" (Matthew 7:22–23).

From Jesus's response, we can conclude that these ministers, prophets, and Christian workers were never joined with Him or knew Him, regardless of what was proclaimed or demonstrated.

Could you imagine being married to someone for many years and performing all the acts and duties associated with marriage, and then the other person says on your death bed that he or she never knew you? All activities and intimacies equate to nothing? Imagine the shock this would deliver.

Just as the scripture says man shall leave his parents and cleave to a wife and the two become one, Christ desires that the church of believers be one as the Father and He are one (John 10:30; John 17:11, 21–22). This oneness is more than just agreement; it is one in identity. God commands a husband to love his wife as his own flesh. In other words, God wants man to see his wife as he sees himself in affection.

When someone says they don't know you or tells another you were never known, this indicates no fellowship or relationship took place. Jesus said He would say to those professing great work in His name that they never really met, never became acquainted, never knew one another as friends, never had fellowship, never became one, and never agreed in thought. This presents a huge problem for the so-called believer. Philippians 2:7-8 indicates, Jesus earnestly prayed to the Father that, as Philippians 2:7–8 indicates, He earnestly prayed to the Father that the body of believers would become partakers in their oneness (John 17:11, 21). Do you believe in this oneness? It takes faith to believe.

What is this faith? Faith is a substance. Faith must be in the Word of God. Jesus is the Word made flesh (John 1:12, 14). In order to have faith, one must hear and receive with full assurance and conviction the inspired Word of God. Trusting in a pastor or fellowship, no matter how gifted or accomplished is not solely true faith in God. Churches can have relevant programs for all ages with evidence-based outcomes, be financially prosperous but still be lacking in a true hunger for God resulting in the testimony of the church of Ephesus in Revelations 2:4.

Could professed faith be lessened to connotations and proclamations, never coming to true spiritual connection, having a form of godliness? The answer is yes.

A good son or daughter does not use one's birthright as a platform to gain influence, power, and authority to manipulate. Such behavior from a child is embarrassing, disappointing, disrespectful, selfish, ungrateful, insubordinate, and hurtful. Such misuse causes shame to a family name. Some so called Christians give Christianity and God a bad name.

Many may say, I have healed the sick, laid hands on people, and delivered may from poverty, hopelessness, and other trying circumstances. Will Christ say, "Depart from me ye workers of iniquity; I never knew you. (Matthew 7:22-23)

It is written, he said to them, my house will be called a house of prayer, but you are making it a den of robbers. (Matthew 21:13)

Let no one deceive you by any means; for that day will not come unless the falling away comes first, and the man of sin is revealed. (2 Thessalonians 2:3 New King James Version)

For Christ sent me … to preach the gospel: not with wisdom of words, lest the cross of Christ should be made of none effect. For the preaching of cross is to them that perish foolishness; but unto us which are saved it is the power of God (2 Corinthians 1:17- 18) New King James Version)

Now, is the judgment of this world; now shall the prince of this world; now shall the prince of this world be cast out. And, I if be lifted up from the earth – I will draw all men unto me. (John 12:32 New King James Version)

CREATE A CLEAN HEART

In my heart, You write a song:
Many pleasures have come my way.
Superficial they are, and in Your Word I want to stay.
I see Your beauty in a day.
I see Your blessings that way.
I feel strong from Your touch.
You bring me joy 'cause You loved me that much.
As a young woman, I stand,
seeking and desiring to be
Guided by Your hand.

CREATE A CLEAN HEART

We communicate with God in our hearts. With each wonder and recognition of miracles, desire your heart to be more transformed into a glimmer of His light. Our heart is where we related to God and He with us. I believe this is the reason King David asked God for a clean heart (Psalm 51:10).

In Luke chapter 8, Jesus is teaching the parable of the sower. He compared the Word of God to being like seeds to be planted in good soil (fertile ground). He referenced an open heart ready to receive and nurture the Word which establishes God's character. The account of Matthew 13:2–9 shows Jesus teaching His disciples heart conditions are like different types of soil, with some seeds (the Word) falling on ground not fully receptive, thus hindering the Word from being fully effective. Every minister who preaches, and every person who prepares to listen, should pray for open and receptive hearts to receive, to retain, and to produce spiritual fruit as a result of the hearing. By doing so, the Word will be planted in good soil (fertile heart) as the Bible instructs, able to bring forth fruit (John 15:1-5). It is indeed a waste of time to be exposed to something and not be able to apply or demonstrate its principal worth.

Since the heart can hinder receiving the full benefit of the Word, then it is important to deal with its condition. There is a blessedness in knowing hurts, disappointments, and things out of control can be given to God, examined in and healed by the Word. A clean heart can be achieved this way. When criticized or mistreated, a person must give hurts to God while examining oneself in regards forgiving others. The heart in these instances remains untouched.

When examining oneself, it is important to use the right magnifying glass (God's Word). This ensures not only accurate judgment, significant correction, and certain chastisement, but also plenteous mercy. Hallelujah! Similarly, this principle can be applied when praying for others and listening to burdens. A Christian must have a clean heart. One cannot judge or take sides. All that is heard and perceived must be placed back in God's hand through prayer. (Galatians 6:1) This is not easy; it requires a spirit of meekness and faith. A dear evangelist and mentor explained the importance of these traits many times. Create in us, O Lord, a clean heart whether we are listening to learn, praying to lift up concerns, or bearing burdens to support a brother or sister.

King David knew and understood the importance of a clean heart. After sinning with Bathsheba, he acknowledged that sin separates, and that he needed restoration and divine support. The king also asked for this provision before explaining God's ways to others. Notice in Psalm 51:1–13 that David also asked for mercy, to be washed thoroughly from iniquity. He acknowledged that he had sinned against God and that God was justified in His anger. David asked to be purged, to have joy again, and not be casted from the presence of God. He asked for a free spirit. Then he promised to teach transgressors God's way.

> I will sing unto the Lord as long as I live: I will sing praise to my God while I have my being. (Psalm 104:33, New King James Version)

> Bless the Lord, O my soul, and forget not all his benefits: Who forgiveth all thine iniquities: who healeth all thy diseases. (Psalm 103:2–3, New King James Version)

> He hath not dealt with us after our sins; nor rewarded us according to our iniquities. For as the heaven is high above the earth, so great is his mercy toward them that fear him. As far as the east is from the west, so far hath he removed our transgressions from us. Like a father piteth his children, so the Lord piteth them that fear him. (Psalm 103:10–13, New King James Version)

> Keep thy heart with all diligence; for out of it are the issues of life. (Proverbs 4:23, New King James Version)

> Thy word have I hid in mine heart, that I might not sin against thee. (Psalm 119:11, New King James Version)

> Search me, oh God, and know my heart, try me, and know my thoughts see ways. (Psalm 139:23, King James Version)

Galley Up and Go—
Don't You Dare Faint

I am going through, and it doesn't look like I'm winning.

All show of hands and evidence seems to dictate I'll lose.

My back is up against the wall.

Enemies are looking for my downfall.

My flesh and sin within me take my enemies side.

All hands down—in my flesh, I could hide.

But if I don't face up and face it and fight,

All Satan's angels disguised as light will dance at midnight, rejoicing over my defeat that I chickened out and did retreat.

Then my Father will not get the glory from my professed love and devotion to Him. (Guess what? He'll always be glorified!)

"I have never seen the righteous forsaken nor his seed begging for bread."

I'll lean on, climb, and trust in Jesus instead.

I'll pray my mind stays on Him. "He that keeps his mind on me I'll keep in perfect peace."

I'll tell my disappointments, failures, resentments, and hurt that Satan wants to build a fortress with "Satan, the Lord rebuke you." Then the Lord will release me from every bondage.

GALLEY UP

The race is not given to the swift nor to strong but to the one who endures until the end. (Ecclesiastes 9:11)

While psychological causes are still debated, my observation is that procrastination often stems from fear. Fear of what? Fear of failure, of not meeting or exceeding expectations, of the responsibility that often comes with success. Whatever the case, procrastination is a dreadful thing. I have been called a person who is always preparing to get organized. I never quite get there, but the pursuit never dies. For me, it is exhilarating to start a project, but through the process interest fades, and the project goes unfinished or is put on the backburner. Once, a manager to whom I reported provided feedback to her direct manager that I lacked follow-through. She never directly shared her evaluation with me. Fortunately, my manager's boss was impressed with my abilities and felt I was promotable, and she cared enough to share her observations. At first the words stung because they were true. I knew it but did not know others observed that I struggled in this area. Rarely can people tell you things about yourself you don't already know.

Bringing things out into the open is good because you are rarely fooling others. Those courageous enough to confront you deserve much gratitude. Wisdom should instruct you to appreciate them; you are better because of their confrontation. Remember scripture tells us the Lord chastises those whom He loves (Hebrews 12:6). Often when faced with obstacles, we quit or find it easier to say, "I am bored," "I can't," or "it's impossible," and we do not continue.

In 2 Chronicles 20, King Jehoshaphat was faced with more trouble than he could imagine, and he became afraid. He did not understand the reason the Moabites and Ammonites came against Judah so strongly, when God had been merciful and not allowed Judah to harm them in a previous confrontation. These nations in turn rewarded Judah by coming into alliance against them. While afraid, Jehoshaphat did know to humble himself, cry out, and ask the Lord for help. He cried out in desperation, "We have no might against this great company that cometh against us; neither know we what to do but our eyes are upon thee." Just as Jehoshaphat cried out to God regarding the children of Moab and the children of Ammon, we also must cry out to God regarding any opposition faced: be it our own weaknesses, human enemies, or any spiritual opposition. We must tell the Lord we do not know what to do, but our dependency is upon Him. He gives us guidance and strength to obtain victory. When we do this, the same result Judah and Jerusalem experienced will be our outcome. They believed God and were established. Stop procrastinating. Follow through. Finish the task. Galley up and go!

Do not fret not thyself because of evil men neither or be thou envious against workers of iniquity. (Psalm 37:1 New International Version)

While we look at the things which are seen: for the things which are seen are temporal; but the things which are not seen are eternal. (2 Corinthians 4:18 New International Version)

Though I sit in darkness—Lord will be my light. (Micah 7:8b New International Version)

Men ought to always pray, and not to faint. (Luke 18:1 New International Version)

CYPRESS SWAMP DILEMMA

Feet dried and cracked from walking in the desert.
Toes that have sunk into quicksand and ache from the sucking power below.
Swampy branch and weeds, nestled in the hell, cry from useless tow.
A predicament one finds himself taken captive in, not by his will.
A cypress swamp dilemma.
Reoccurring weaknesses that meet you in the morning when you wake.
A pitiful countenance and life full of mistakes.
A rebellious spirit restless because it cannot get what it wants;
It knows no peace, even entangled in covetousness. The spirit is arrested by thieves.
A Christian who has made two steps and stalls at a critical point,
open for fruitless takeover.
A cypress swamp dilemma.
Fleshly desires that rule the body but make the heart and mind sick,
Like quicksand in the belly and thorns in the flesh, prickly prick.
Nauseous in mind from confused thoughts because we don't obey.
Seeking wisdom from the dead and foolish counsel—a destiny to dread
results in generations of dismay.
A cypress swamp dilemma.
Twisted gifts and fake calls roaming through the day and night,
Stalled in procrastination, hindered by all shapes of frights.
A prophet who will not tell the truth, pleasing people while the earth around them decays.
A cypress swamp dilemma.

Cypress Swamp Dilemma

God can change destinies. Pray to Him and praise Him!

You can be neck deep in dung, sinking in a swamp of confusion, and recall that nothing is impossible with God. Nothing is too hard! These truths will immediately transport an open heart into a refreshing waterfall of comfort.

I am not exactly sure where first I heard the phrase "cypress swamp dilemma," but as young girl, everything perceived as not quite right was referred to a cypress swamp dilemma. It even became a joke between me and my sister, who desperately wanted me to find another phrase to describe what I perceived. Though younger, she had always been able to quickly decipher things. At the tender age of three, she was direct and curious about words used.

"Now, what exactly is a cypress swamp dilemma?" It is a situation where one feels stuck, like one is sinking or tangled up. The further predicament is that there seems to be absolutely no way out, with no human help to rely upon. *Webster's* definition is below.

cypress (noun)—scaly leaved evergreen trees and scrubs

swamp (noun)—spongy wetland with mire, morass and marsh

dilemma (noun)—undesirable or unpleasant choice

You get the vision: trees and scrubs in a wilderness surrounded by wetland, in which you could sink into the marsh. This is not a pleasant campsite but rather an imagery of being lost and surrounded with no place to go in the wake of impending danger.

In Psalm 69, King David prayed to God. In his prayer, you can hear despondency because he was overwhelmed. David confessed that he was sinking because he had cried until his throat became dry. Everything looked so bleak, and he perceived his enemies were greater than the number of hairs on his head. King David was certainly familiar with dilemmas, but he also was intimate with a God of miraculous deliverances. We see his dependence and confidence as he wrote.

> If it had not been for the Lord who was on our side now may Israel say; If it had not been the Lord who was on our side, when men rose up against us: Then they had swallowed us up quick, when their wrath was kindled against us: Then the waters has overwhelmed us, the stream had gone over our soul: Then the proud waters had gone over our soul: Blessed be the Lord, who hath not given us as a prey to their teeth. Our soul is escaped as a bird out of the snare of fowlers: the snare is broken, and we are escaped. Our help is in the name of the Lord, who made heaven and earth. (Psalm 124:1–8)

Bruce Wilkinson's "Prayer of Jabez" made the prayer in 1 Chronicles 4:10 famous. Many have heard of the book and have prayed the prayer of Jabez with great expectations, even unbelievers. The scripture indicates Jabez was given a name with destiny to bring sorrow. Jabez believed the God of Israel could intervene and change destiny, and so he prayed to that end. "Oh that thou wouldest bless me indeed, and enlarge my coast, and that thine hand might be with me, and that thou wouldest keep me from evil, that it may not grieve me!"

If you find yourself in a 'cypress swamp dilemma', the poem might describe your feelings. My recommendation is to follow Jabez's example and King David, with an expectancy of deliverance. Finally, meditate on the words of the following scriptures.

> He that dwelleth in the secret place of the most High shall abide under the shadow of the Almighty. (Psalm 91:1 King James Version)

> Surely he shall deliver thee from the snare of the fowler, and the noisome pestilence. He shall cover thee with his feathers, and under his wings shalt thou trust: his truth shall be thy shield and buckler. (Psalm 91:3 King James Version)

> Rejoice not against me, O mine enemy: when I fall, I shall arise; when I sit in darkness, the Lord shall be a light unto me. (Micah 7:8 New International Version)

> God is our refuge and strength very present help in trouble. (Psalm 46:1 King James Version)

> The Lord of hosts is with us; the God of Jacob us our refuge. Selah (Psalm 46:7 King James Version)

For thou wilt light my candle: the Lord my God will enlighten my darkness. For by thee I have run through a troop: and by my God have I leaped over a wall. As for God, his way is perfect: the word of the Lord is tried: he is a buckler to all those that trust him. For who is God save the Lord? Or who is a rock save our God? It is God that girdeth me with strength, and maketh my way perfect. He maketh my feet like hind's feet and setteth me upon my high places. (Psalm 18:28–33 New International Version)

Jabez cried out to the God of Israel, "Oh, that you would bless me and enlarge my territory! Let your hand be with me and keep me from harm so that I will be free from pain. (1 Chronicles 4:10 New International Version)

WOUNDED SIDE OF JESUS

Like a fox and its hole,
Can I hide it in Your side? What? This earthen vessel—me.
I can't lie: sometimes I get afraid and want to hide;
The temptation, I can't deny.
Once I feel the anointing of Your sweet touch, who wants to go back into this world's twisted thrust?
I love and need You oh, so much.
I'm just a rib that wants to retreat.
Living water and redeeming blood flows from the spout within—so glad it purchased and made me next of kin.
You said I'd stay here until You call me home; until then, at times I feel I just roam.
Oh, it sounds kind of wimpy, but it's true: I want to nestle up to Your wounded side, push in my head, pull the body in, wrap up, and hide.
There I'll be safe. I know this to be true. Not a part of this world or even man's body, but attached only and fed thoroughly by and within You.

WOUNDED SIDE OF JESUS

Disciples ran from the Calvary in fear. Today, disciples and all humankind must run to it in faith.

Mel Gibson's Passion of the Christ was used to depict the physical sufferings of Christ. Viewers were able to see vivid screens of Christ's beating and crucifixion. This was a dramatic presentation of the sufferings of Jesus Christ. He endured being mocked and beaten for people who could care less and had no understanding of the necessity and significance of his sacrifice (Isaiah 53:3-9). As compelling as the motion picture was, we did not see and cannot know the spiritual side of the sufferings of Christ. Prior to taking man's punishment, He did not know separation from the Father and had not experienced God's wrath on sin. He simply knew no sin or spiritual darkness, yet He became this defiled thing called sin for humankind.

> Who being in the form of God, thought it not robbery to be equal with God: But made himself of no reputation, and took upon him the form of a servant, and was made in the likeness of men: And being found in fashion as a man, he humbled himself and became obedient unto death, even the death of the cross. (Philippians 2:7–8)

> He was wounded for our transgressions and bruised for our iniquities the chastisement of our peace was upon him and with his stripes we are healed. (Isaiah 53:5 New International Version)

One of the most moving scenes in the movie was when the soldier went to finish off Jesus by piercing Him in the side with a sword. Upon this piercing, water and blood came out. The movie showed a significant spray of water that gushed in the soldier's face. At that moment, praise swelled up in me as I held my seat. Right there in the theater, I remembered Jesus's invitation: "If any man thirst, let him come unto me, and drink. And, Jesus told the woman at the well the water I have for you will ensure you to never thirst again" (John 4:14). Jesus is the living water. He tells believers, "He that believeth on me as the scripture hath said, out of his shall flow living water" (John 7:38). We are washed by water, which is the word of God and cleansed by Jesus Christ's blood (Ephesians 5:26; Revelation 1:5; 1 John 5:8).

This precious blood was shed for all humankind and was a fulfillment of Old Testament prophecies and predictions (Revelation 5:9). There was yet another side of the spiritual suffering endured, which was experienced by God's beloved Israel, whom the Father cut off for a period of time to bring Gentiles into relationship with Him. Israel was a chosen people to have an intimate relationship with the Father. Israel's temporary estrangement is due to of lack of faith, according to scripture (Romans 11:7; Romans 20:25).

> Israel was holiness unto the Lord, and the firstfruits of his increase. (Jeremiah 2:3)

> He came unto his own, and his own received him not. But as many as received him, to them gave he power to become the sons of God, even to them that believe on his name. (John 1:11 New International Version)

> For I would not, brethren, that ye be ignorant of this mystery, lest ye should be wise in your own conceits; that blindness in part is happened to Israel, until the fullness of the Gentiles be come in. (Romans 11:25 New International Version)

Let us not focus only on the crucifixion. A great resurrection occurred. Come along and climb into His side with me. Partake of spiritual rebirth, and let's await our bodily resurrection.

And They Overcame the Enemy by the Blood of the Lamb

When Satan wants your mind, he's trying all the time.
He wants you to be confused. He's counting on that you will lose.
He will use the flesh to put you to the test.
He knows just who and what to use. He's betting that you will choose him.
From God-like thoughts he wants you to stray.
With your lips, anything that tears down, he'll use you to say.
The uttermost farthing you will pay, he hopes.
With the weakness of your flesh, he'll throw you into a frenzy.
Among his tricks, he has plenty.
When Satan wants your mind, he's striving all the time to get you in his grips.
He'll use the hunger of a harlot's hips or the flattering use of an unwise lip.
He will stoop down hard and roll you low.
There is no way, no place, nowhere—to no limits he won't go,
Just to hear you cry.
And from God's plan he wants to hear you shy in disbelief.
That old fool, that old thief.
He'll even try imaginations and other motifs.
His goal, his plan is continual regret and eternal grief.
Fact is, there is only one relief.
The dependent, trusting, leaning, and impending, all-imposing,
Completely exposing precious blood of Jesus.

Overcame by the Blood of the Lamb

In a time of great heaviness, I was thinking of all that seemed to be against the world, the body of Christ, and me. The Lord interrupted my pity party. He reminded me of the finished work of the cross. The redemption of humankind came through the shed blood of Jesus Christ. "Without shedding of blood is no forgiveness of sin" (Hebrew 9:22b).

In our churches, and in gospel and inspirational music, we hear chants that talk too much about the devil stomping on his head, letting him know you are encouraged, making him mad, telling him you aren't playing with him, and even blaming or rebuking him when things go wrong. All that sounds fine and good, and we enjoy the catchy tunes and snap phrases. Even in sermons, we hear litanies on telling the devil he must stop this or that, can't steal this or that, cannot have this or that.

What did the scripture say to do? Are we to be concerned about making the enemy mad as opposed to pleasing God? How did Jesus address the enemy? Jesus addressed him with the word of God. He addressed him on the efficacy of Himself – Lord over all (Matthew 4:4). Jesus is the Word made flesh (John 1:14). No other railing accusation was brought against satan. Michael, the archangel of the Lord who had been in hand to hand combat with the devil and his fallen demons, answered him one way: the Lord rebuke you (Jude 1:9). Be aware of things that come to trip up, snare, or destroy. The Word says do not be ignorant of the enemy's devices. I am not implying not to take authority over, or not to stand in the authority Christ gave. But there is a proven way to address the enemies' work. No political movement and no cute little songs can do the work. The enemy has already been defeated. He's already defeated! Why do we continue give applause and attention to a defeated foe? Faith in the finished redemptive work of the cross should be a reminder of his destiny and position. The devil was created, then defeated. Shouldn't we take Jesus Word and work as a prescriptive and defeat him? For no one outdid Satan but Jesus (Revelation 12:11; Luke 10:17).

Let's look at a proven ways from the Word this is to be done. Michael, the archangel who fought Lucifer and his angels in heaven, found it *not necessary* to bring all types of accusations or condemnations against Satan when Satan contended with him regarding Moses's body. He simply said, "The Lord rebuke thee." Remember that Michael is the same angel who will reappear in the tribulation time to assist Israel. Michael has a high heavenly position with great responsibility and authority from God, yet he only said, "The Lord rebuke thee" (Jude 9; Deuteronomy 34:6; Genesis 3:1; Revelation 12:7–9).

In Zechariah 3:1–2, the Lord showed Zechariah a vision of the high priest Joshua interceding on behalf of Jerusalem, and of Satan standing close at his side to oppose the work. The Lord humbled the enemy by saying, "The Lord rebuke thee." He affirmed that Jerusalem was His chosen ones and that the Lord Himself had plucked Jerusalem out of the fire. He did not need to give a long litany or long chant. He simply said He chose Jerusalem and put the enemy in his place.

It is also interesting to note that in the vision, Joshua himself was clothed in filthy garments, but that did not matter. The Lord commanded the angels to change his attire, which indicated cleansing, and the placing of holy garments on him, depicting righteousness. For the reason of the Messiah's coming and selection of Israel, the people were not to be harmed or hindered from their rightful position. Joshua was literally standing in the righteousness of Christ Jesus, as we do today.

In Matthew 4, after Jesus fasted, Satan was allowed to tempt Him two times. The third time, Jesus rebuked him and told him to get away. Each time Satan offered Jesus something, and he even tempted Him to obey him by referencing God's promises of protection. Jesus spoke only the Word of God, reprimanding and reminding him that He simply obeyed, listened to, and lived because He bowed to only the one true and living God. Speak the Word only! Jesus said,

> Man shall not live by bread alone, but by every word that proceedeth out of the mouth of God … It is written again, Thou shalt not tempt the Lord thy God … Get thee hence, Satan: for is written, Thou shalt worship the Lord thy God, and him only shalt thou serve. (Matthew 4:1-10)

In other words, Jesus rebuked him. Rebuke is a correction. When one is rebuked, one is put back in line. Jesus reminded Satan with His word that he was in no place to offer Him anything. He was and had all that was needed: The Lord. And the Lord rebuked him. He overcame the enemy howbeit, prophetically by His own blood.

> And they overcame him by the blood of the Lamb, and by the word of their testimony. (Revelation 12:11 New International Version)

> Woe to inhabiters of the earth and of the sea! For the devil is come down unto you, having great wrath, because he knoweth that he hath but a short time. (Revelation 12:12 New International Version)

And the dragon was wroth with the woman, and went to make war with the remnant of her seed, which keep the commandments of God, and have the testimony of Jesus Christ. (Revelation 12:17 New International Version)

The thief cometh not, but for to steal, and to kill, and to destroy: I am come that they might have life, and that they might have it more abundantly. (John 10:10 New International Version)

For this is my blood of the new testament, which is shed for many for the remission of sins. (Matthew 26:28 New International Version)

ANOINTING PLAYS ME

THE ANOINTING PLAYS ME

Being in the presence of creation had to be a wonder and awe inspiring—the explosion of the creative power within God. No, not a big bang—things cluttering around. Then they just hung themselves in their proper place. For that foolishness, there is no time, no thought, no room, no space.

When God called the world into being, it immediately began to obey and bring its objects together. Colors began to match, and seeds and obits began to detach. All of this universe had to strike it's it, against it's at, and make a match. For light had to come forth when He spoke it! And it came quickly. The divider of division had to separate day from night, and the adder of pluses joined to blend it all together. Mathematician, scientist, and artisan—on a mission. Such splendor! Creating the whats and ifs to bring together mountains, valleys, streams, oceans, and cliffs. Dotting all i's and crossing all t's. The anointing of the breather, moving creation from time and space. All for us, a section, a part, a place—making the seed and commanding it to reproduce after its replica to trace its origin. Oh, I imagine the splendor.

And for money to purchase its wealth, there is no lender, only from the purchase of His tender, loving kindness and absorbent mercies. Play me like a piano and beat me like a drum, sing from me like a clarinet. When your finger touches me, I hum. I am—yes, I am, just as one of Your miraculous awesome works You have already done, just the feeling You give to me, if for but a moment. I dance with my fingers across these keys, and with my finite mind, I want to fly and soar far beyond the sky because You write a lovely song in my heart. "Lord, let us never part." On the splendor of Your touch, make me whine like a baby, shy like an old woman awaiting sweet rest. O Lord, put me to the test to make sure that I love You in my heart. Let us never, ever part. Your anointing sways me. Let me never betray thee. Your anointing for all my days BE. Work it into a melody. Just let the anointing play me!

ANOINTING PLAYS ME

Writing poetry makes me imagine being an old, dilapidated piano experiencing a complete refurbish of the finest pieces of ebony and ivory, then being polished with premium oils and being played by Beethoven.

"Anointing Plays Me" is a signature poem. It is one of my favorite pieces. I use the metaphor of God's people as instruments, pieces of clay. Its focus is the Lord. And if God's finger of love does not play and mold our clay, there will be no music. There are special times when the Holy Spirit fills us with the magnitude of His greatness. It is in this place where the greatest revelation is revealed. A brother in Christ once shared, "If you have been blessed enough to receive a revelation, don't get cocky; realize there is still so much more." His words bear witness to 1 Corinthians 13:9–10. Getting inspired or receiving revelation reminds you that God is mindful of you and seeks a relationship of sharing.

Writing poetry about the Lord feels smooth as the sound of a string being laid gently upon a harp. In the moments God inspires, nothing else and no one else matters. Surely this is a peace that passes all understanding. If you have never had a sweet visitation from God's Spirit, you are missing the core of this existence. It is an awesome experience!

> O Lord, how manifold are thy works! In wisdom hast thou made them all: the earth is full of thy riches. So is this great and wide sea, wherein are things creeping innumerable, both small and great beasts. These wait all upon thee; that thou mayest give them their meat in due season. That thou givest then they gather; thou openest thine hand, they are filled with good. Thou hidest thy face, they are troubled: thou takest away their breath; they die and return to dust. Thou sendest forth thy spirit, they are created: and thou renewest the face of the earth. (Psalm 104:24–25, 27–30 New International Version)

How It Feels to Be Inspired

You just breathe on me then—I cannot hold it. I feel I could scream.
On Your strength I need to lean, for I cannot—no, no, do anything,
O Your Majesty, without You.
You said You have more for me, but if Your power hit me with the
fullness, I see and I know I'd truly, truly leave here, and this place
would be a far memory at best.
Oh, then put me to the test and be not afraid, for what You cause me
to write, I know that again of tonight: that You are there and here
with me. And no, I am not afraid. I have Your company, and I swear
no words You can give me to describe this to human morality. Neither can
they ever feel that which I cannot even fathom, this Holy Ghost
by Your spirit that lives in and breathes through me. I know for sure I belong
to You!

How It Feels to Be Inspired

Once in line for prayer, I could feel a gentle breeze nestle around the bottom of my dress. My dress tossed gently back and forth. I knew regardless of who touched me, or who was around, I was already in His presence. I lifted my head up, arched my neck, and looked at no man, expecting to receive from no one other than the Lord. Suddenly, upon my face I felt and smelled the softest, sweetest air. The Lord had breathed upon me. I shall never forget how that felt.

I always wished I could sing or have a well-trained voice. My alto voice can be really strong and supportive in choirs with other altos on both sides, in the front, and in back of me. Together, we can form a strong alto section. Despite voice lessons my range, pitch or tone varies as a soloist. Although I do not know how it feels to be used as a singing voice like an instrument, I do know what it feels like to get an idea that is so beautiful that I know it is solely from God. I also know how the anointing feels and have been trained to understand when it is present, when the moment is over. I also know how it feels and have been trained to understand when the anointing is present, and when the moment is over. This too I feel is important.

Apart from me you can do nothing. (John 15:5 New International Version)

For in him we live, and move, and have our being. (Acts 17:28 New International Version)

I will instruct thee and teach thee in the way which thou shalt go: I will guide thee with mine eye. (Psalm 32:8 New International Version)

HE'S ALL OVER ME, AND HE'S KEEPING ME ALIVE

Don't you dare let that moment slip away
When you hear a still quiet voice tell you,
Come. I want to spend time with you.
Draw nigh unto me, and I will draw nigh unto you.
When he says I love you and am so enveloped in everything that you need,
I think about it night and day.
I long to protect you and will show you everything you need to know.
I will direct you to the correct places to go, and when I'm quiet, I want you to be still
And wait on Me.
For when My love is silent, there is a purpose, you see.
You have no inkling of how much I care, but the depth of My devotion
You can't fathom, so don't you try, don't even dare. Your understanding is much too brittle.
You can't even touch the wealth of the overflow—you don't understand such.
I wait for you to tell me you need Me daily.
I watch you go to and fro, but I still send angels to surround you though.
When you feel my stillness, stop immediately and come.
Go talk to Me, for I require your commitment. Can't you see?
If you love Me, then feed my sheep. It's not a formula or theological deep.
Draw nigh unto Me, and I will draw nigh unto you.
You're My handmaiden, and I am working around, through, and in you.

HE'S ALL OVER ME

Picture an old country church deep in the crevice of a valley. Listen closely to the melody flowing from its steeple, filling the basin like ocean waves tossed back and forth by a hurricane. Though strong and roaring, it somehow gently croons, "He's all over me and keeping me alive." The trees on the mountaintops that stand towering alongside begin to wave in affirmation as their branches clap, and leaves fall gracefully to the ground only to pop up straight. Imagine that the rocks and boulders start to sweat like big drops of tears as they prepare to cry aloud. Every living creature within its sound humbly confesses.

An old gospel song says, "He's all over me and He is keeping me alive." As a child, I vividly remember church mothers and elderly people singing that song during morning devotions. Looking at their frail bodies, I understood why they sang the song with much conviction. After watching them sing each chorus, those seemingly useless bodies evolved into a confident stern strength.

I became convinced regardless to what my eyes perceived, every word from their lips was witness to their claim. Their age and the condition of their bodies demonstrated that God was all over them and was indeed keeping them alive.

Do not cast me away when I am old; do not forsake me when my strength is gone (Psalm 71:9 New International Version)

Yet, O Lord, you are our Father. We are the clay, you are the potter; we all are work of your hand. (Isaiah 64:8 New International Version)

And even the very hairs of your head are all numbered. So don't be afraid; you are worth more than many sparrows. (Matthew 10:30 New International Version)

Three Parts of Us

Ever feel divided or conflicted?

You think your mind has been transformed, then you conform.

You wonder what part can perform.

Feels like a perfect storm – all within your being.

Makes you want to go fleeing—but then, there is nowhere to flee from yourself.

Is it because you don't understand?

In our humanness – this us, we lack in-depth study of the original plan, man is placed in a body.

He is given a soul, so you know—a spirit so you can unite with Him.

I laid on a couch. An enemy as a spirit came through the wall, walked right into my room.

All of me would have been consumed in fear.

Except a spirit from within arose and shifted the atmosphere. It hovered and claimed ownership!

I looked to see. Recognized who I was.

My soul recognized, "that's me." My body lay helpless because I was detached. An evil spirit that challenged the family thought it had prey to jump on and land. The spirit of God within me usurped the plan.

My spirit arose and fought for this clay, this shell, this soul, this mind - my life. The spirit within me began to reprimand the enemy. "You must go!" I recognized my spirit. My soul recognized me. This shell. I had no fear, you see.

There was no worry. No need to hurry. No need to fight. The spirit within me declared God's Word. It took he, the roamer to Himself by Calvary, then put him that destroyer to flight. He scurried out just the way he came. I take no credit. He had to GO in Jesus's name!

THREE PARTS OF US

Body—flesh, self, carnal aspect of man

Soul—mind, consciousness, and thoughts

Spirit—heart, inner man, hidden man of the heart

The spirit man is the part of man that is like God. For God is a spirit and must be worshipped in spirit and in truth (John 3:6). This spirit, the Holy Spirit, which is God's Spirit, is what God sent to live within the believer. This is the inner man and cooperates with the heart. For this reason, King David prayed, "Create in me a clean heart and renew a right spirit" (Psalm 51:10). The other parts of man that don't get saved or regenerated are the body (flesh) and the soul (mind). Romans 12:12 says, "Be not conformed to this world but be ye transformed by the renewing of your mind." The mind and thoughts are changed by the Word of God. The flesh, which is the body, is crucified through application of the word of God and through fasting. It is important to get the Word of God in your mind to gain God's perspective. The Word of God is powerful, sharp, and cuts down into man's core (Hebrews 4:12–13). The word of God discerns man's thoughts and intentions, and when received in faith, it changes man's mind. Jesus work first changes our minds, then our hearts, and then our hands. The sin nature that remains in the body wars against the law of the mind (Roman 7:21-25). In other words, the carnal mind harbors thoughts and can be motivated to sin when it has not been changed or regenerated (Romans 7:23–24). The fact that body and soul await full redemption is also joined by the fact that the whole world waits for this adoption—the redemption of the body. Romans 8:22–23 and 1 Corinthians 15:44, 50–54 speak to the necessity of a coming change for the total man and the earth. The reason this must be accomplished is that flesh and blood cannot inherit the kingdom of God. If after salvation all parts of man were completely redeemed and pure, there would be no need for a change of body as Jesus promises in Luke 6:43–45.

The apostle Paul prayed for the Thessalonian church that God would sanctify them wholly (fully) – spirit, soul, and body. He prayed the church to be preserved blameless unto the Lord's coming (1 Thessalonians 5:23). This work could only be done by the sanctification. The church was to be set apart from a corrupted world.

Man is a spirit. His soul lives in a body. The heart can be cleansed (Psalm 51:10). Only the spirit of man is saved (Romans 8:11, John 4:24) (Romans 12:2). The work of the flesh must be crucified by the Word of God (Galatians 5:24; Galatians 2:20).

The following things need to be done with the Word of God:

1. Read it. (Begin with Psalms, Proverbs or the Gospel of John)
2. Apply it to every situation.
3. Let it reveal the work of the flesh, the old nature and its desires within you.
4. Repent and cast off the work of your flesh.
5. Pray for the strength to apply the word to your life.
6. Pray for God's perspective (*to be your own*) to see and hate all sin -- just as He does for its destructive impact.
7. Call all things to meet the truth of the Word regardless to what you see and feel.

In the world we live, we are constantly being taught and enticed by our own feelings, social media, advertisements, and friends. We are taught that we owe this flesh something. "Go ahead; you deserve it." "You need this." "You must have this or that." These thoughts even invade faulty biblical teachings. Yet the Word of God tells us that we owe the flesh nothing (Romans 8:12 New International Version).

This body will die, and it is dying daily. If all your focus is on a dying thing, what else valuable is there?

> The spirit of a man is the essence of his life: "body without the spirit is dead." (James 2:26 King James Version)

In the beginning, the Spirit of God moved upon the earth, which was void of order and productivity. When God separated dark from light, created everything, and set it in order, He formed man from the dust of the ground and breathed into him—man came alive (Genesis 1:7). But he did not become alive until God blew His breath into man's nostrils. This breath was spirit. Man was made in the image of God. God is a spirit, and those who worship Him must do so in spirit and in truth (Genesis 1:26; John 4:24).

A quickening of spirit affirms that God cannot be sought or worshipped just in the soul or the body. The spirit must worship Him, the spirit of Christ Jesus, within the believer. The soul can desire Him. The body can be disciplined and brought into obedience to serve Him. The actual power to perform His will is given expressly by His spirit (John 4:23–24), and that spirit is alive in the believer.

Spirit of Freedom - Freedom of Spirit

They're looking in all the wrong places!
Losing time and taking up spaces
As the wind blows so freely—free liberty in spirit completely.
Freedom of spirit releases dependability on mind, emotion, body, anything physically.
Free liberty means rooting up and tearing down in your inner man,
Which is done through the Word of God
Spirit of freedom is the gift of liberty for those who accept and meditate on Him.
His standard is holiness, by release of personal will.
Be molded like pottery, never dry, rock hard in the heart.
Free liberty praise—still!
Bending and shaping in the soul of the inner man.
Freedom of spirit by the creator, ordainer, master of the universe, preparer of the Promised Land.
Free liberty is in His spirit, speak freely with other tongues, laying on of hands.
Faith in the Lord Jesus Christ alone.

Deliverance for all who have succumbed.

SPIRIT OF FREEDOM—
FREEDOM OF SPIRIT

If God was not holy and able to transform us into His likeness, what would be the point of worshipping Him?

Victory for the Christian must come through recognition and acknowledgment that God desires to develop holy people. A personal desire for holiness and an awareness that holy living can be obtained. This can be accomplished by a submitted life. The Lord transforms our desires. He gives the faith to rely upon Him to perform His holiness in us. A desire to approach and please God on one's own merit is a futile effort (Hebrews 12:14; Romans 8:7-8).

First of all, no man on his own merit has the right to approach God. Accepting this fact, we recognize we do not have to be holy or clean in and of ourselves. The fact is we are not holy or clean. Man is sinful and corrupt by nature. There is no gift or penitence man can give a holy God. Jesus Christ was the only sacrifice acceptable to be offered as a substitute for man's unfit spiritual condition (Hebrews 10:10–12). God Himself prepared a sacrifice and instituted His provision for man to have a means by which to approach Him (Hebrews 10:5).

No legalistic behavior, right motive, or self deprivation justify man enough to approach God. "Come as you are" (Isaiah 1:18; Isaiah 55:1; Revelation 22:17). While yet in sin, Christ died for all men and women. This fact alone provides foundation for a gospel, whereby a loving God looked upon the condition of a lost humanity deprived of peaceful relationship with Him. He rescued us from wrath, separation, and a destiny of eternal damnation. Jesus Christ, the Son of God, became a sin offering for sinful world. As a result of His sacrifice, all can come boldly to the throne of grace for the express purpose of obtaining mercy. This gift of mercy ensures we do not get what we deserve, which the Bible refers to eternal damnation and separation from the Father. Jesus Christ took the penalty for us and we stand in his righteousness (Romans 3:21-31; 6:23).

With that established, God is the only one able to present us holy and righteous before Himself (Jude 1:24). According to scripture, this is done by the offering of his Son as the only acceptable sacrifice. Because of Jesus's work on the cross, a believer is declared righteous. With this acceptance, a believer should desire to examine oneself in God's Word, apply it to the heart, and yearn to obey it fully. Christ alone allows us to stand in a holy place. His mission is to present the body of believers holy and without blemish.

> As Christ also loved the church, and gave himself for it; that he might sanctify and cleanse it with the washing of water by the word, that he might present it to himself a glorious church, not having spot or wrinkle, or any such thing; but that it should be holy and without blemish. (Ephesians 5:25–27, King James Version)

> Thou art neither cold nor hot: I would thou wert cold or hot. (Revelation 3:15, King James Version)

> Thy testimonies are very sure: holiness becometh thine house, O Lord, forever. (Psalm 93:5, King James Version)

> But as He who called you is holy, you also be holy in all your conduct, because it is written, "Be holy, for I am holy." (1 Peter 1:16, King James Version)

> God is a spirit, and those who worship Him must worship in spirit and in truth. (John 4:24, King James Version)

"For if we would judge ourselves, we should not be judged. But when we are judged, we are chastened of the Lord, that we should not be condemned with the world. (1 Corinthians 11:31–32, King James Version)

SHAMMAH

I am crying to you for help.
My back is against the wall.
My spirit shouts for me,
"Shammah."
Crackles through my throat say, "Shammah."
He says, I hear.
I say, Shammah, I hear you.
Shouts burst from of my spirit: Shammah!
He answers;
I calm down,
am completely comforted.
Shammah, I hear you, I say.
Be still,
Come nigh.
You have been assured the Lord is there with you.

SHAMMAH

While kneeling and crying out to God, suddenly a keen awareness overtook me that Jehovah Shammah was present and His ears were open to my cry. It is a comfort when you cannot cry or speak a word to know God is there—Shammah.

As Israel would identify Jehovah Shammah, I recognized Him. I called upon Him in my spirit and felt His presence and peace. I praised Him with my hands lifted in awe of the privilege of His visitation. Even so, I did not fully understand what it meant that He was actually present.

We often find it time-consuming or burdensome to pray then wait for God to speak back to us. We should recognize and press diligently toward those moments. It is a privilege. Embrace prayer time. Through Jesus Christ, we have received access to enter into the holy place where we can approach the throne of grace. It is an honor and privilege to humbly come before His throne (Hebrews 4:14–16).

Have you ever been so enamored with people that once you were in their presence, you did not ask anything but just smiled and were comforted? I have, and they would finally have to ask what they could do for me.

It is an honor to be in the presence of an Almighty God. Sometimes it is good to simply bask in His presence. There is no better comfort. When you love Him and want to be in His presence, He will certainly tell you to ask what you want (Matthew 6:33).

When you cry out for help and touch God by faith, you will discover He is Jehovah, Shammah, the Lord. He will be there, present and available.

> And the name of the city from that day shall be, The Lord is there. (Ezekiel 48:35b New International Version)

> For we do not have a high priest who is unable to sympathize with the feeling of our weaknesses … Let us then approach the throne of grace with confidence so that we

may receive mercy and find grace to help in time of need. (Hebrews 4:15–16 New International Version)

Let us draw near with a true heart in full assurance of faith. (Hebrews 10:22 King James Version) THE LORD IS THERE. (Ezekiel 48:35 New King James Version)

SELAH

God's Word be true.
Let God's Word abide in you.
Eat the Word;
Put it in your mouth.
In season and out,
From God's Word never deviate or doubt.
Selah, amen.
From impossible situations, He can.
Selah, amen.
Shammah,
I hear you.
Selah,
He can.
Selah,
When autumn becomes winter,
He can plant flowers as if it were spring,
Bursting with fresh, new things
Because Shammah is present.
Selah,
Amen.

SELAH

And having done all to stand, stand—and having said much, represent.

When you see the word *Selah* written at the end of a verse in Psalms, it means "so be it" and "amen." Selah was used as a musical rest to indicate you should stop and think about what was just said or heard. Often we quickly breeze through scriptures. When someone asks what is meant, we say it is self-explanatory or it means just what it says. Well, it does mean just what it said. The more relevant issue is, do we know and understand what it said fully and what it meant? The phrase "having a form of godliness but denying the power" comes to my mind. Paul's assessment of Israel also bears mandate for self examination:

> For I bear them record (Israel) that thy have a zeal of God, but not according to knowledge. For they being ignorant of God's righteousness, have not submitted themselves to the righteousness of God. (Romans 10:2-3)

The next time you read any verse of scripture, imagine "Selah" after it. Stop and think about every word that proceeded. What do they mean all together? Take time to cross-reference and note where it may have been referenced previously and refer to footnotes. What is being emphasized? Who and to whom is the text speaking, and regarding what? The bottom line is to think about it, eat it, and digest it (Jeremiah 15:16).

Scripture tells us to study to show oneself approved by rigorous study to ensure the Word of truth is divided and applied in an appropriate manner. Studying and examining yourself is a good thing. The only thing more important is to seek the Holy Spirit, whom Jesus promised in John 14:26.

Some of the Holy Spirit's work is to teach, remind, and unlock understanding. Selah and Shammah are appropriate conclusions.

I hope Autumn: The Mantle Lifted introduced poems, thoughts that connected with you; moreover, my prayer is the scriptures be firmly planted in your hearts, grow to bear fruit as you lift your purpose in Christ and prepare for the harvest. I say to you "Shammah", the Lord is present. And, "Selah", Amen. Think about both!

In Christ the promises of God are "Yes", and through Him, Amen 2 (Corinthians 1:20).

The promises of God are yeah and amen. Selah.

A BORROWED BREATH

Who Are You?
God breathes life into every nostril – Genesis 2:7

What difference does your breath make?

_____

_____

_____

_____

_____

_____

_____

_____

_____

_____

_____

_____

_____

_____

_____

QUICKEN MY SPIRIT

What did God Do for Your Spirit?
- In Him, we live, move and have our being, we his offspring - Acts 17:28

_____

_____

_____

_____

_____

_____

_____

_____

_____

_____

_____

_____

_____

_____

_____

_____

_____

THE ANOINTING PLAYS ME

We are God's handiwork. We are to spread His aroma everywhere
among those saved and those perishing.

Have you asked God to let His anointing play you? In other
words, can God have His way with you?

Let's thank Him in advance for working in you and me what is well - pleasing
to Him – Ephesians 2:10, 2 Corinthians 2:15, Hebrews 13:21

_____

_____

_____

_____

_____

_____

_____

_____

_____

_____

_____

_____

_____

_____

If you are not a Christian, you may recite a sinner's prayer and be saved.

God loves you.

John 3:16. For God loved the world so much that he gave his only Son, so that everyone who believes in him will not perish but have eternal life. You can turn your life over to God's control because he loves you and wants the very best for your life. In fact, he loves you so much that he gave his Son, Jesus, to die on this cross for you. When you turn your life over to him, you are giving your life to the One who knows you inside out. Don't you agree this is good place to put your trust?

Sin keeps you from having a personal relationship with God.

1 John 3:4. Everyone who sins is breaking God's law, for all sin is contrary to the law of God. It is difficult for many to understand the concept of sin. We live in an amoral world that believes each person can decide what is right, what is true, and what is "moral" – whatever means based upon different appetites. God does have standards about right and wrong. There is such a thing called sin". The bible says, "everyone has sinned." All of us! We simply cannot help it – we're human. Sin gained permission to enter the humanity through Adam and Eve.

All people are born sinners

Romans 5:17. For the sin of this one man, Adam, caused death to rule over many. Sin leads to death. That's a big problem! Sin is why all of us die naturally. God is perfect, he cannot have anything to do with sin. Sin entangles and prevents a personal and peaceful relationship with him (Isaiah 59:22). As a matter of fact, sin's consequence even robs us of peace in the world, within ourselves and with others.

Romans 3:23. For everyone has sinned; we all fall short of God's glorious standard.

What's so bad about sin?

Roman 6:23. For the wages of sin is death. God desires to have a loving relationship with all men. He desires to give us, not only natural life but spiritual life. This spiritual life only comes from a personal relationship with God. Some people find it difficult to understand having a "relationship with God. Yet it is possible through his Son, Jesus Christ.

Why Jesus Christ?

John 14:6. Jesus told him, "I am the way, the truth, and the life." No one can come to the Father except through me. Due to sin, God could have nothing to do with man. This was made clear in the Old Testament. God's plan all along was to send his Son, Jesus – a perfect being to be the final an ultimate sacrifice to our sin.

Jesus died to take on the penalty our sins deserved. He took our punishment. Because of Jesus, a way is prepared for us to able to have a personal relationship with a holy God.

1 Peter 3:18. Christ suffered for our sins once for all time. He never sinned, but he died for sinners to bring you safety home to God. He suffered a physical death, but was raised to life in the Spirit.

You can respond with belief in Christ.

Romans 10:9-10. If you *Confess* with your *Mouth* that Jesus is Lord and **Believe** in your *Heart* that God raised him from the dead, you will be saved. For it is by believing in your heart that you are made right with God, and it is by confessing with your mouth that you are saved. You simply need to believe. That doesn't mean that you don't have any questions or that you understand everything. It simply means you recognize a need for a savior.

Hashtag #BHCM

Believe in your Heart. Confess with your Mouth. You shall be saved.

Next steps after confession.

After you confess Jesus Christ as Lord, the bible gives instruction to be baptized (Mark 16:16). He that believeth and is baptized shall be saved; but he that believeth not shall be damned.

Salvation means a new life.

All men were born as sinners and that sin separates us from a relationship with God. Man needs a way for sin to be taken away. Man needs to be given a new life. Jesus Christ died a sinners death and was raised into a resurrection for this new life. This new life is for you (Romans 6:3-4). Do you not know that all of us as were baptized into Jesus Christ were baptized into his death? Therefore, we are buried with him by baptism into death: that like Christ was raised up from the dead by the glory of the Father, even so we also should walk in the newness of life.

What else? You need to join a community of believers.

Anytime something new is started. People do better in a community of believers that can strengthen and encourage the decision. The bible tells people not the neglect assembling together with other believers. It asserts the word of God shared with the encouragement of a community of believers strengthens resolve. This is important to those who have a mindset on growing stronger in relationship with God (Hebrews 10:25). The Apostle Paul pleaded with the Ephesian church. His pleading was for all denominations, the new and mature believers.

"As a prisoner for the Lord, then I urge you to live a life worthy of the calling you have received. Be completely humble and gentle; be patient, bearing with one another in love. Make every effort to keep the unity of the Spirit through the bond of peace. There is one body and one Spirit, just as you were called to one hope when you were called; one Lord, one faith, one baptism; one God and Father of all, who is over all and through all and in all" (Ephesians 4:1-6).

[Excerpts: Life Application Study Bible NLT, A Christian Worker's Resource]

Share your experience of **Autumn: The Mantle Lifted**

Join the community, connect with the author and other readers!

www.mantlelifted.com